CHINESE BREEZE

Learn with Ease

2

Love it!

Chant it!
Rhyme it!

Tap it!
Clap it!

Act it!
Rap it!

Speak it!
Write it!

Learn with a Smile

Jian Gao

Illustrated by Eric Keto

ISBN   978-1-940031-11-8

Printed in the United States of America

ACKNOWLEDGEMENTS

Thank you to all the students I was fortunate to work with at Belmont Hill School of Massachusetts. You are full of wonder, insight and imaginations. You are my sources of inspiration.

Table of Contents

What are the Chinese characters in these pictures?

A Chinese character often represents
a part of history, an image or idea, or an attitude about life.

Word for Word   a pair - bamboo - thunder - to fly - to be stuck
many people - tears - a well - hot - rock pile

Let's see how many you can get right.

1 泪	2 卡	3 雷	4 炎	5 双
6 众	7 竹	8 井	9 飞	10 磊

Chinese Breeze 2: Scope & Sequence

Unit	Topics	Theme Connection	Grammars
1	开学啦!	Classroom expressions School subjects	1. Reviews: The past tense 2. The resultative complements 3. The action-measure words: 遍，次
2	时间	Telling the time Favorite activities	1. The future tense: 要，会，快要， 2. Wh-words: 几，哪 3. Basic word order: time 4. The adverbs: 就，才
3	别担心。	Morning routines Clothes & Accessories	1. Sequence: 先，然后，再，最后 2. The use of 不然，要不是 3. The adverbs: 又，再，还 4. The verbs: 穿，戴
4	多少钱?	Chinese currency & Stores Negotiate a better price	1. Asking the price: 多少钱？怎么卖？ 2. Wh-word: 怎么 3. The use of 能，这么，那么
5	大小多少	More Adjectives The Comparisons	1. The use of adjectives 2. The comparison: 比 3. The use of 跟…一样，更，最
6	以前 & 以后	Rooms in a house Various activities	1. The position words 2. The use of: 有，是，在 3. The use of 以前，以后
7	你看怎么样?	Asking for opinions Giving suggestions	1. The use of 又…又… 2. The use of 更，最，要不 3. The use of 长得，长得像
8	真的吗?	Feelings & Complaining Family issues	1. The resultative complements 2. The use of 让 3. The use of adjectives
9	我病了。	Body parts Illnesses Giving advice	1. 哪儿不舒服？ 2. _____不舒服。 3. The Simple directional complements 4. _____了没有？
10	我饿了。	Chinese food & Fruits Order food & drinks	1. The complex directional complement 2. Review: The alternative question 3. The use of 什么都
11	天气	Weather Outdoor activities	1.The use of when: …的时候 2. Adverbs: 太，非常，特别 3. _____怎么去？
12	交通	Places in town Transportation & Directions	1. Asking for directions: _____怎么走？ 2. The use of 往，朝 3. 附近有_____吗？
13	中国	Facts about China Cultural taboo	1. The past perfect tense: 过 2. The use of 如果

Unit	Key Words	#
01	开学，站，起来，下去，注意，听，用，心，记，问题，举，该，**安静，大声，出去，** 作业，数学，已经，完，加，等于，课文，念，遍，历史，报告，写，纸，科学，实验，结果，心肠，留，玩	34
02	时间，上午，中午，下午，晚上，半夜，号，几点，放学，就，告诉，休息，才，**小时，刻，分，半，差，钟头，** 忙，快要，死，从…到…，晚，开，小说，划船，唱歌，健身，火锅，电视，歇，**遛狗，逛街，钓鱼，打扑克，网络，游戏**	38
03	背心，上衣，毛衣，T-恤衫，衬衫，大衣，内衣，汗衫，裤子，衬裤，内裤，牛仔裤，迷你裙，连衣裙套裙，衣服，帽子，鞋，袜子， 担心，点儿，洗脸，刷牙，煎蛋，不然，又，骂，懒，着急，分钟，绝对，来得及，洗澡，穿，剩下，到，糟糕，忘，	38

04	钱，分，毛，块，元，角，人民币，港圆，美元，加元，英镑，欧元，日圆，银行，换钱 杂志，手表，怎么，那么，贵，能，便宜，老外，会，砍价，刷卡，现金，挣钱，花钱，时髦，名牌，大号，中号，小号	34
05	高，矮，胖，瘦，重，轻，香，臭，绳，伞，冷，深，浅，容易，难，酸，甜，清淡，咸 多…，俩，一样，比，哥俩，姐俩，更，最，穷，富，聪明，笨，随和，挑剔，帅，丑，内向，外向	37
06	上面，下面，书架，左边，右边，前面，后面，房子，里面，房间，外面，旁边，中间，对面，公园，阁楼，地下室，洗手间，公寓，以前，以后，饭厅，厨房，切，客厅，练，卧室，生日卡，收拾，先，花园，兔，然后，打扫，浴室，车库，得，整理	38
07	怎么样? 显得，特，神气，土气，戴，挺，老气，眼镜，书生气，拎，皮包，倍，傻气，一举一动，孩子气，看起来，项链，领带，跳舞，又…又…，围巾，亮，觉得，够，漂亮，粗，脖子，细，难看，怎么办，要不，下棋，去你的，小气，大方，热心，倔	38

Unit	Key Words	#
08	好像，开心，生气，做错，题，难过，坏，害怕，被，教练，烦恼，驾照，感到，尴尬，生化，吃惊，走，着，假， 惹，公平，位置，二手，货，玩具，汽车，算啦，让，老二，认，**家务活**，**老大**，**老小**，**偏心**，**独生子**，**独生女**，**唠叨**，**地位**，	38
09	双，放下，伸出，肩，踩，蹦，跳，弯下，身子，摸，脚趾，直，摇，脑袋，往，退，座位，**屁股**，**背**，病，疼，嗓子，咳嗽，拉肚子，发烧，舒服，没用，冰淇淋，**痛**，**量**，**体温**，**体重**，**医院**，**过敏**，**失眠**，**肥胖病**，**急诊室**，**看急诊**，	38
10	饿，炒饭，包子，饺子，辣，汤，宫爆，鸡丁，米饭，渴，咖啡，汽水，**请客**，**买单**，**春卷**，**豆腐**，**付钱**，**吃素**，**随便**， 水果，当然，鸭梨，橘子，菠萝，香蕉，桃子，葡萄，芒果，李子，樱桃，草莓，椰子，木瓜，杏子，信，尝，**生**，**熟**，	38

Unit	Key Words	#
11	天气，晴，露营，行，雨，攀岩，雪，下雪，预报，温度，阳光，阴天，凉爽，风，雾，多云，阵雨，毛毛雨，冰雹， 时候，...时候，海边，泰山，骑马，市内，下雨，坐车，游，山上，种树，乡下，散步，刮风，扫路，特别，烧烤，郊游，夏令营，	38
12	交通，到处，转，十字路口，四面八方，东，西，南，北，银行，广场，地铁，邮局，商场，图书馆，超市，教堂，迷路，问路， 上班，机场，车站，打车，搭车，跑，直走，拐，摩托车，公车，电车，火车，三轮车，船，飞机，票，远，近，附近，	38
13	入乡，俗，禁，如果，送礼，沏茶，递，毛巾，名片，满，整，烟，照办，当面，道谢，师傅，麻烦，先生，太太， 筷子，放，鞭炮，爬，长城，古老，遥远，东方，仔细，像，公鸡，朝，尾，民族，汉族，文化，地理，民俗，	38

485

School is more than making the grade. It is a place for finding out what you like to do, trying out new ideas, and having fun! Pay attention to your teacher's voice. Chances are it will get louder when he or she is talking about something you really need to understand.

zhàn qǐ lái   zuò xià qù
站 起 来！坐 下 去！

zhàn qǐ lái   zuò xià qù
站 起 来！坐 下 去！

líng xiǎng la   shàng kè la
铃 响 啦，上 课 啦！

qǐng zuò hǎo   bié shuō huà
请 坐 好！别 说 话！

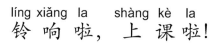

ná chū shū   ná chū bǐ
拿 出 书！拿 出 笔！

zhù yì tīng   yòng xīn jì
注 意 听！用 心 记！

yǒu wèn tí   qǐng jǔ shǒu
有 问 题，请 举 手。

gāi shuí la   gāi wǒ la
该 谁 啦？该 我 啦！

lǎo shī   lǎo shī   líng xiǎng la
老 师，老 师，铃 响 啦，

lǎo shī   lǎo shī   xià kè ba
老 师，老 师，下 课 吧！

Key words

1	开学	kāixué	school starts
2	站	zhàn	to stand
3	起来	qǐlái	to get up
4	下去	xiàqù	to get down; to get off
5	注意	zhùyì	to pay attention to
6	听	tīng	to listen; to hear
7	用	yòng	to use
8	心	xīn	heart
9	记	jì	to remember
10	问题	wèntí	question; problem
11	举	jǔ	to raise; to lift
12	该	gāi	should; must
13	该谁啦?	gāi shéi la	Whose turn?
14	请安静。	qǐng ānjìng	Be quiet, please.
15	大声说。	dàshēng shuō	Speak aloud.
16	出去!	chūqù	Get out!

If you like to play Lego…

 Many ideas, thoughts and feelings are expressed by combining two or more characters to form a new word, such as 电脑 computer, literally means "electric brain". In a way, each Chinese character is like a Lego brick.

Let the words flow!

Are you stressed about your homework? Are you daydreaming while studying? Homework isn't that hard. Working efficiently is half work and half psychology.

nǐ zuò yè zuò le méi yǒu
你作业做了没有?

zǎo zuò hǎo le　zài zhè er　nǐ kàn
早做好了。在这儿,你看:

shù xué zuò yè yǐ zuò wán　yī jiā yī děng yú sān
数学作业已做完,一加一等于三。

yīng yǔ zuò yè yǐ zuò wán　kè wén niàn le qī bā biàn
英语作业已做完,课文念了七八遍。

lì shǐ bào gào yǐ xiě wán　wǔ zhāng zhǐ　qī dà duàn
历史报告已写完,五张纸,七大段。

kē xué zuò yè yǐ zuò wán　shí yàn jié guǒ zài shàng mian
科学作业已做完,实验结果在上面。

nà nǐ de hàn yǔ zuò yè ne
那你的汉语作业呢?

hàn yǔ lǎo shī xīn cháng hǎo
汉语老师心肠好,

méi liú zuò yè yào wǒ wán er
没留作业要我玩儿。

zhēn de ma　bú huì ba
真的吗?不会吧。

Key words

1	作业	zuòyè	homework assignment
2	数学	shùxué	math
3	已经	yǐjīng	already
4	完	wán	to finish
5	加	jiā	to add
6	等于	děngyú	to be equal to
7	课文	kèwén	text
8	念	niàn	to read aloud
9	遍	biàn	A measure word indicates the frequency of an action verb.
10	历史	lìshǐ	history
11	报告	bàogào	report; to report
12	写	xiě	to write
13	纸	zhǐ	paper
14	科学	kēxué	science
15	实验	shíyàn	to experiment; experiments
16	结果	jiéguǒ	result
17	心肠	xīncháng	heart
18	留	liú	to give (homework)
19	玩	wán	to play

Language Focus

1.1 Vocabulary Review.

Read it aloud. Translate it into English.
Write it in Chinese characters, and say it aloud again as you write it.

	English	Chinese
1. 别站在这儿。	_____	_____
2. 坐好!	_____	_____
3. 上课别说话。	_____	_____
4. 请拿出课本。	_____	_____
5. 大家注意听。	_____	_____
6. 用心做题。	_____	_____
7. 该你们啦!	_____	_____
8. 我已经做完了。	_____	_____
9. 没写历史报告	_____	_____
10. 实验结果呢?	_____	_____
11. 热心肠	_____	_____
12. 没留作业	_____	_____
13. 来我家玩儿吧。	_____	_____
14. 不会吧!	_____	_____

Learning vocabulary is an essential part of learning a language. The more vocabulary you know, the more you will be able to understand what you hear and read; and the better you will be able to say what you want to when speaking or writing. So, review your vocabulary frequently.

1.2   Grammar Review：The imperative sentence

An imperative sentence expresses a request or command. In Chinese, the word order of an imperative sentence is exactly the same as the word order in English.

For example:　　　　请坐下。　　　　　　请举手。
　　　　　　　　　　Please sit down.　　　　　　Please raise your hand.

In Chinese, 请 must be placed at the beginning of an imperative sentence.

1. Do your homework.　　　　　　　　_____

2. Sit over there, please.　　　　　　_____

3. Pay attention to what I say.　　　　_____

4. Please don't feed this bird.　　　　_____

5. Don't touch my computer!　　　　　_____

1.3   Body Language.

When you are sitting in a class, what do your actions say about your attitude? Take a look at the pictures below. Now put yourself in a picture and think of what your body language might say to your teacher.

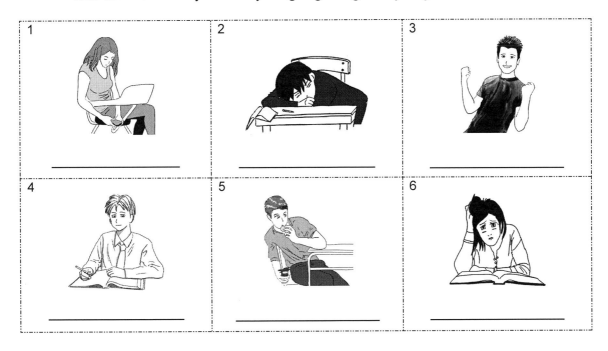

1.4 Grammar Review: The past tense

Although Chinese does not have verb conjugations as in many other languages, there are ways to express past actions.

When the particle "了" is placed after a verb, it shows an action happened in the past.

Question:　1. Subj. + verb + 了 吗?　　　老师来了吗？

　　　　　2. Subj. + verb + obj. + 了 吗?　你做作业了吗？

　　　　　3. Subj. + verb + obj. 了 没有?　你做作业了没有？

　　　　　4. Subj. + verb + 了 + obj. 没有?　你做了作业没有？

　　　　　5. Subj. verb + 没 + verb + obj.?　你做没做作业？

Answer:　　1. Subj. + verb 了.　　　　　我做了。

　　　　　2. Subj. + verb + obj. 了.　　　我做作业了。

　　　　　3. Subj. 没（没有）verb + obj.　我没（有）做作业。

1. Did teacher Li give us homework?　　_____

2. My friend bought a new guitar.　　　_____

3. How come you didn't go with them?　_____

4. Why didn't you write the report?　　_____

5. Do you know who ate my hotdog?　　_____

6. They didn't come to school today.　　_____

Study often and in small time periods. Four half-hour study periods are usually more effective than a two-hour block. Your attention span in Chinese is not as long as in your native language. Study and listen to the recordings everyday, even if it is only for 5 minutes.

1.5 Grammar: The resultative complements

Unlike English, verbs in Chinese do not indicate the result of actions. When you want to indicate the result of an action, a resultative complement is placed after an action verb. Please remember only stative verbs and verbs can be used as resutative complements.

Here are the stative verbs or verbs used as resultive complements.

好	properly; in a proper way 坐好，拿好，做好，写好，想好	上课了，请大家坐好。
会	to master a skill 学会，	我学会了开车。
见	to have seen; heard 听见，看见	我听见有人说话。

到	1）to have done something
	    找到，买到，收到
	
	2）to reach a place, a time, a level
	    看到，学到，走到，听到，做到
		我找到了书包。
		
		我们学到了第三课。

完	to finish 看完，吃完，做完，写完，说完	做完作业再玩儿吧。

Fill in the blanks with the proper word given.

1. 记者没有找_____他的车。　　　　　　(会，到，完)

2. 这孩子三岁就学_____了滑雪。　　　　　(见，到，会)

3. 我听_____老师在叫我们。　　　　　　　(好，见，完)

4. 上课啦！请大家坐_____。　　　　　　(好，完，会)

5. 他吃_____了一只北京烤鸭！　　　　　(会，见，完)

6. 我还没想_____买什么车呢。　　　　　(到，好，会)

1.6 Grammar: The use of 完 and 好

When you want to indicate the result of an action, a resultative complement is placed after a verb of action. 完 and 好 both indicate that the action has completed.

For example: 我吃完了晚饭。 I finished my dinner.

　　　　　　　我做好了作业。 I finished my homework.

1. Have you finished writing your history report?

_____

2. Can I watch TV? I've already done my science experiment.

_____

3. Dinner is ready. Let's have dinner.

_____

4. I don't think I can finish reading this book.

_____

1.7 Describe the pictures using 完，好，会，到，见

1.8 Grammar: The action-measure complement

When counting the number of times an action is repeated, an action-measure word 遍 or 次 will be used. It always appears after the action verb, and is referred to as a verb complement.

遍 biàn: happened once through

For example:　　　　这本小说我看了三遍。
　　　　　　　　　　I read this novel three times.

　　　　　　　　　　请你再说一遍。
　　　　　　　　　　Please say it again.

次 cì: happened once

For example:　　　　我给你打了两次电话。
　　　　　　　　　　I called you twice.

　　　　　　　　　　北京我只去过一次。
　　　　　　　　　　I only went to Beijing once.

Fill in the blanks with 次 or 遍.

1. 那家饭店我去过一_____。

2. 我来教室找过你好几_____了，可是你都不在。

3. 老师要我们每个汉字写五_____。

4. 这本书写得真棒！我还想再看一_____。

5. 美国学生可以考几_____SAT?

6. 这个星期我妈只给我打了一_____电话。

7. 高老师要我们每天听三_____课文。

8. 这本书看一_____就不想再看第二_____了。

9. 跟你说了多少_____了，你怎么还去找她！

1.9 Grammar: The use of 会

会 huì – to know how to

For example: Affirmative: 我会说汉语。   I can speak Chinese.

         Negative: 我 <u>不会</u> 说汉语。   I cannot speak Chinese.

       吗 - question: 你 <u>会</u> 说汉语吗？   Can you speak Chinese?

  Affirmative-negative: 你会不会说汉语？   Can you speak Chinese or not?

会 huì - more likely (indicate possibility)

      A: 他夏天会去上海吗？   Is he going to Shanghai this summer?

      B: 我想他不会。   I don't think he will.

1. I think he will look for you.   _____

2. Do you think she will go to France?   _____

3. He knows how to cook fish.   _____

4. Can your younger sister ski?   _____

会不会？

1.10 Reading & Speaking

What's Your Study Style?
Everyone has a learning style that works best.
Circle the answer that describe you, and share it with your friend.

	选择题
1	A. 我喜欢一个人学。 B. 我喜欢跟朋友一起学。 C. 我喜欢在教室里学。有问题我可以问老师。 D. Or_____
2	A. 我最喜欢上数学课，因为我喜欢我的数学老师。 B. 我最喜欢科学课，因为我喜欢做实验。 C. 我最喜欢上英语课，因为我喜欢看小说。 D. Or_____
3	A. 我喜欢看着电视做作业。 B. 我喜欢吃着小吃做作业。 C. 我喜欢一边上网一边做作业。 D. Or_____
4	A. 我常做完作业再玩儿。 B. 我常玩儿完再做作业。 C. 我早上起来做作业。 D. Or_____
5	A. 我喜欢老师问我问题。 B. 我喜欢问老师问题。 C. 我老是坐在教室后面。 D. Or_____

1. 你最喜欢学什么？为什么？　_____

2. 你最不喜欢学什么？为什么？　_____

3. 什么样的老师是好老师？　_____

1.11 Fun with Chinese characters

A Chinese character often represents a part of history, an image, an idea or an attitude about life.

For example, the character for fresh is 鲜, which consists of two parts: 鱼 (fish) on the left side, and 羊 (sheep or goat) on the right side. So, the character 鲜 suggests "fresh and delicious" taste.

It is said that every Chinese character contains a picture. So, use your imagination when studying Chinese characters. Have fun!

讠	Write down the characters with 讠 in it.
讠 is related to speech or language. It is always placed on the left side.	
攵	Write down the characters with 攵 in it.
攵 refers to the moment of the hand. It is usually placed on the right side of a Chinese character.	

1.12 word detective Not so new

Here are some basic Chinese characters you have learned.
Let's see if you can decode their meanings.

	Pinyin	English	Make a sentence
1. 听话	_____	_____	_____
2. 记住	_____	_____	_____
3. 想念	_____	_____	_____
4. 留心	_____	_____	_____

1.13 Law and Order.

If you were a teacher, what rules would you lay down?

1 上树	2 在教室跑	3 在教室里玩儿
4 上课用手机		5 在教室吃泡泡糖
6 带狗来学校	7 上数学课写汉字	8 Add your own

Culture Focus

1. What are some of the things you learn when you learn Chinese as a foreign language?

_____

2. Body language is an important part of nonverbal communication, and is closely connected with culture. Noticing the signals that people send out with their body language is a very useful social skill. Compare Chinese body languages to the body languages in your culture.

As long as you know your numbers, telling time in Chinese is easy. Here is a fun rhyme to help you learn. So, rhyme it, clap it, and rewrite it!

zǎo shàng　　shàng wǔ　　zhōng wǔ
早 上 ， 上 午 ， 中 午 ，

xià wǔ　　wǎn shàng　　bàn yè
下 午 ， 晚 上 ， 半 夜 。

jīn tiān jǐ yuè jǐ hào　　jīn tiān xīng qī jǐ
今 天 几 月 几 号？ 今 天 星 期 几？

xué xiào jǐ diǎn fàng xué　　wǒ xiǎng wèn wen nǐ
学 校 几 点 放 学？ 我 想 问 问 你。

jīn tiān sì yuè wǔ hào　　jīn tiān xīng qī yī
今 天 四 月 五 号， 今 天 星 期 一。

liǎng diǎn jiù fàng xué　　wǒ lái gào sù nǐ
两 点 就 放 学， 我 来 告 诉 你。

xiàn zài jǐ diǎn le　　wǒ xiǎng wèn wèn nǐ
现 在 几 点 了？ 我 想 问 问 你：

jǐ diǎn zuò zuò yè　　jǐ diǎn qù xiū xi
几 点 做 作 业？ 几 点 去 休 息？

xiàn zài yī diǎn le　　wǒ lái gào sù nǐ
现 在 一 点 了， 我 来 告 诉 你。

wǒ qī diǎn zuò zuò yè　　bàn yè cái qù xiū xi
我 七 点 做 作 业， 半 夜 才 去 休 息。

zǎo shàng　　shàng wǔ　　zhōng wǔ
早 上 ， 上 午 ， 中 午 ，

xià wǔ　　wǎn shàng　　bàn yè
下 午 ， 晚 上 ， 半 夜 。

Key words

1	时间	shíjiān	time
2	上午	shàngwǔ	morning
3	中午	zhōngwǔ	noon
4	下午	xiàwǔ	afternoon
5	晚上	wǎnshàng	evening
6	半夜	bànyè	midnight
7	号	hào	date; number; size
8	几点	jǐ diǎn	What time is it?
9	放学	fàngxué	School is over.
10	就	jiù	just (It indicates an action that happened too early.)
11	告诉	gàosù	to tell
12	休息	xiūxi	to take a break; to rest
13	才	cái	not until (It indicates an action that happened too late.)
14	小时	xiǎoshí	hour
15	刻	kè	quarter / 一刻 = 15 minutes 三刻 = 45 minutes
16	分	fēn	minute; points; to divide
17	半	bàn	half
18	差	chà	lack of; to fall short of
19	钟头	zhōngtóu	a colloquial word for hour

Let the words flow!

Limit your activities after school so that you'll be able to finish your homework. Setting a timer for each activity you do may help you be more productive.

nǐ máng ma
你 忙 吗?

zhōu mò ne
周 末 呢?

nǐ máng shén me ne
你 忙 什 么 呢?

kuài yào máng sǐ le
快 要 忙 死 了!

kuài yào máng sǐ le
快 要 忙 死 了!

wǒ cóng zǎo máng dào wǎn
我 从 早 忙 到 晚!

wǒ cóng zǎo máng dào wǎn
我 从 早 忙 到 晚!

wǒ yī diǎn zuò shù xué   liǎng diǎn xué kāi chē
我 一 点 做 数 学, 两 点 学 开 车。

wǒ sān diǎn xiě bào gào   sì diǎn kàn xiǎo shuō
我 三 点 写 报 告, 四 点 看 小 说。

wǒ wǔ diǎn qù huá chuán   liù diǎn xué chàng gē
我 五 点 去 划 船, 六 点 学 唱 歌。

wǒ qī diǎn qù jiàn shēn   bā diǎn chī huǒ guō
我 七 点 去 健 身, 八 点 吃 火 锅。

wǒ jiǔ diǎn kàn diàn shì   shí diǎn cái xiē yi xiē
我 九 点 看 电 视, 十 点 才 歇 一 歇。

nǐ kě zhēn máng
你 可 真 忙!

Key words

1	忙	máng	busy
2	快要	kuàiyào	almost; nearly
3	死	sǐ	to die; extremely
4	从…到…	cóng…dào…	from…till…
5	晚	wǎn	late
6	开	kāi	to drive (a car, a bus, an airplane, etc.)
7	小说	xiǎoshuō	novel
8	划船	huáchuán	to row a boat
9	唱歌	chànggē	to sing a song
10	健身	jiànshēn	physical exercises
11	火锅	huǒguō	hotpot
12	电视	diànshì	TV
13	歇一歇	xiēyixiē	to take a break; to rest
14	遛狗	liùgǒu	to walk a dog
15	逛街	guàngjiē	to window-shop
16	钓鱼	diàoyú	to go fishing
17	打扑克	dǎ púkè	to play poker
18	网络	wǎngluò	internet
19	游戏	yóuxì	games

Language Focus

2.1 Vocabulary Review.

Read it aloud. Translate it into English.
Write it in Chinese characters, and say it aloud again as you write it.

	English	**Chinese**
1. 现在几点？	_____	_____
2. 上午九点半	_____	_____
3. 半夜回家	_____	_____
4. 今天下午没课。	_____	_____
5. 三个半小时	_____	_____
6. 没做完数学题	_____	_____
7. 咱别告诉老师！	_____	_____
8. 回家休息吧。	_____	_____
9. 两点三刻呢？	_____	_____
10. 大半天	_____	_____
11. 去哪儿划船？	_____	_____
12. 他没学会开车。	_____	_____
13. 忙死我了！	_____	_____
14. 她在写小说呢。	_____	_____

 Planning is the key to making a busy schedule work. Figure out how long it will take you to do each thing – homework, swimming, piano practice, and chess, etc. Then make a plan to get everything finished and stick with it.

2.2 Words used to telling the time.

点 diǎn: o'clock	现在八点。	It is 8 o'clock.
分 fēn: minute	早上八点十分。	It is 8:10am.
刻 kè: quarter	上午十点一刻。	It is 10:15am.
半 bàn: half	下午两点半。	It is 2:30pm.
差 chà: lack of	差一刻九点。	It is 8:45.

Set the Clock

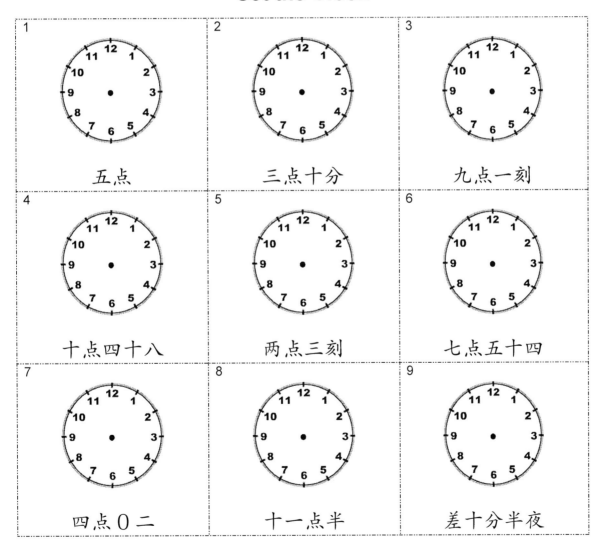

五点	三点十分	九点一刻
十点四十八	两点三刻	七点五十四
四点 0 二	十一点半	差十分半夜

2.3 The World Clock – Time Zones

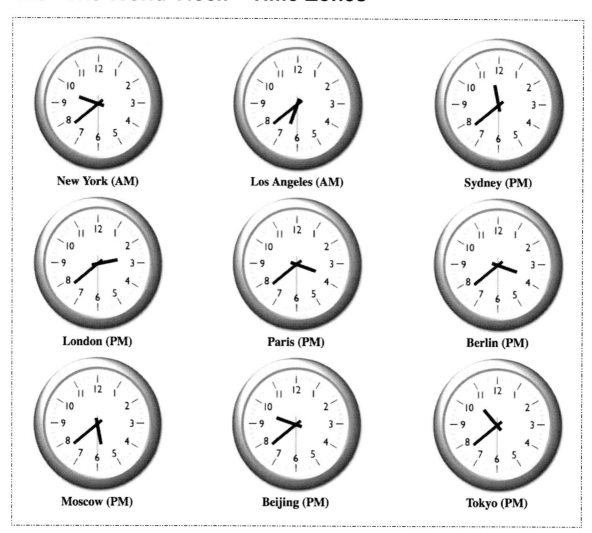

New York (AM)   Los Angeles (AM)   Sydney (PM)

London (PM)   Paris (PM)   Berlin (PM)

Moscow (PM)   Beijing (PM)   Tokyo (PM)

纽约上午九点，北京几点？ 人们在做什么？

1. 纽约： 上午九点，纽约有人上班，有人上学，有人还在睡觉。

2. 北京： _____

3. 巴黎： _____

4. 东京： _____

5. 伦敦： _____

6. 柏林： _____

2.4 Grammar Review: The use of 哪 & 几

年	几年? / 多少年? How many years?		哪年? Which year?
月	几月? What month?	几个月? How many months?	哪个月? Which month?
天	几天? / 多少天? How many days?		哪天? Which day?
点	几点? What time?		
星期	星期几? What day is it?	几个星期? How many weeks?	哪个星期? Which week?

For example: 你想几点来我家?
What time do you want to come to my house?

我想下午三点去你家。
I want to go to your house at 3pm.

Please note:

In Chinese, the time word (when) and location (where) must appear before the action verb. Also, the time word/phrase is placed before the location word/phrase.

For example: 我下午在学校游泳。
I'll swim this afternoon at school.

1. What time did you finish your science experiment last night?

_____

2. Let's play tennis at my house this weekend.

_____

3. When shall we take a break? I'm exhausted!

_____

4. I didn't go to bed till midnight last night.

_____

2.5 The future tense in Chinese.

Please remember that verbs do not change to express tenses in Chinese. Instead, some particles or time words are used to show the tenses.

The following words are used for talking about the future.

1. 要 about to happen

我们要去北京了。
We are going to Beijing soon.

2. 快 (要) going to happen soon

校车快要来了。
The school bus will be here soon.

3. 就 about to happen

我这就去。
I'll go right now.

If a sentence has 明天 or 明年 or 一会儿, you may not need to use any of the time adverbs, such as 要，快要，就要，or 快.

我们明天开车去纽约。
We'll drive to New York tomorrow.

1. What are you going to do this weekend? Do you want to go swimming?

_____

2. Hurry! Class is about to start!

_____

3. Can you be a little faster? The bus is coming!

_____

4. The Chinese New Year is around the corner.

_____

5. We are going to the pet store to get a bird this weekend.

_____

2.6 Vocabulary: The use of 小时 & 时间

小时 xiǎoshí: hour	几个小时? How many hours?	多少小时? How many hours?	三个小时 three hours
时间 shíjiān: time	多长时间? How long?	什么时间? What time / when?	没（有）时间 to have no time

1. I am too busy! I don't have time to play with my friends!

_____

2. We don't have two hours. We only have half an hour!

_____

3. How long did you work on your history report? 5 hours?

_____

4. I am tired. I have been busy from morning till night!

_____

5. Do you have time this evening? Let's watch "Friends".

_____

2.7 My Dream Saturday

You are given the opportunity to design your Saturday's activities. Find out who has a similar dream day among your classmates. Maybe you'll be able to get together sometime.

星期六	吃的	喝的	做的	看的	玩儿的
早上					
上午					
下午					
晚上					

2.8 李超的课表

时间	星期一	星期二	星期三	星期四	星期五
8:20am	汉语	数学	英语	科学	历史
9:05am	数学	英语	科学	历史	汉语
9:45am	牛奶&点心	牛奶&点心	牛奶&点心	牛奶&点心	牛奶&点心
9:55am	英语	科学	历史	汉语	数学
10:40am	科学	历史	汉语	数学	英语
11:20am	自习/问答	自习/问答	自习/问答	自习/问答	自习/问答
12:00pm	午饭	午饭	午饭	午饭	午饭
12:50pm	历史	汉语	数学	英语	科学
1:30pm	音乐	实验	美术	实验	爱好小组
2:20pm	网球	游泳	长跑	健身	放学

你的课表呢？

2.9 The adverbs: 就 & 才

就 is used to express a concept that an action happened unusually "**early**".

For Example:　　　　我今早六点半**就**到学校了。

　　　　　　　　　　I arrived at school at 6:30 this morning.

才 is used to express a concept that an action happened unusually "**late**".

For example:　　　　我昨晚十点**才**做作业。

　　　　　　　　　　I didn't do homework till 10 last night.

1. 校车八点到，丽丽七点一刻_____来等车了。

2. 星期三的报告，李小明今天（星期一）_____写好了。

3. 八点二十上课，谢大山八点半_____起床。

4. 都快半夜了，你怎么_____回家！

5. 石牛三岁_____学会了滑雪。

6. 包小丽晚上八点半_____吃晚饭。

2.10 What a busy October!

十月

星期一	星期二	星期三	星期四	星期五	星期六	星期日
29	30	1 3:10pm 学画画儿	2 6pm 健身	3 7:30pm 舞会	4 4:15pm 看电影	5 8:15am 练唱歌
6 4:35pm 学开车	7 2:10pm 钓鱼	8 3:50pm 骑马	9 1:15pm 看医生	10 6:40pm 看孩子	11 7:30am 做早饭	12 9:15am 去教堂
13 3:30pm 踢足球	14 2:45pm 学开车	15 3:50pm 打篮球	16 3:50pm 学唱歌	17 7:30pm 舞会	18 10:15am 划船	19 12:00 当家教
20 10:50am 历史报告	21 9:35am 科学实验	22 11:15am 数学小考	23 8:30am 汉语小考	24 4:05pm 学开车	25 2:45pm 买吉他	26 9:15am 去教堂
27 4:10pm 健身	28 3:50pm 买糖	29 5:15pm 做晚饭	30 4:05pm 考车	31 6:00pm 鬼节	1	2

你八号下午有时间吗?

那三十号下午呢?

没有，我要骑马。

我要去考车。

Now ask and answer questions with your partner using the information on the calendar.

2.11　Work in pairs.

Talk about each picture with your classmates in class.

你在干什么？

想去游泳吗？

你怎么老是写字？

在**写汉字**呢。

不想，我要写字。

| 1 做火锅 | 2 唱歌 | 3 健身 |
| 4 看电视 | 5 写小说 | 6 Add your own |

2.12　word detective　Not so new

Here are some basic Chinese characters you have learned.
Let's see if you can decode their meanings.

	Pinyin	English	Make a sentence
1. 告别	_____	_____	_____
2. 开夜车	_____	_____	_____
3. 日记	_____	_____	_____

2.13 Fun with Chinese radicals

 A Chinese character often represents a part of history, an image, an idea, or an attitude about life.

For example, the character for star is 星. It consists of two parts:

日 (sun) and 生 (to be born). The Sun is a life-giving star to all stars.

口	Write down the characters with 口 in it.
口 is related to mouth, and is usually placed on the left side or bottom of a Chinese character.	
日	Write down the characters with 日 in it.
日 is related to the sun, and is usually placed on the left side or on the top.	

2.14 Every picture tells a story- - What's yours?

Use your imagination.
Write as many sentences as you can.

1	2	3
	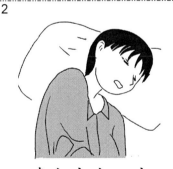	
晚上十点半	晚上十点四十	晚上十一点一刻

1. 你看到了什么？ _____

2. 你听到了什么？ _____

3. 请写个故事。 _____

你好！我叫王小雪，今年十七岁，上十一年级。我不知道你忙不忙，可是，我都快要忙死了！

我每天八点二十上课，可是，我妈六点半就叫我起床了。我爸妈都上班，所以我早上**不但**要给弟弟妹妹做早饭，**而且**还要**送**他们上学。我弟弟妹妹都上小学，妹妹上五年级，弟弟上三年级。

我每天从早忙到晚。我八点二十到一点三十五上课。我今年**选**学五门课：英语，数学，美国历史，化学和汉语。我觉得化学最难学，因为有好多东西**需要**记。历史课的作业最多，老师**常**要我们写报告。我的汉语老师心肠好，所以汉语作业不太多。我每天**差不多**都要做三个多小时的作业。

除了上课，我还有很多**活动**：我周一下午三点健身，周二下午四点半练唱歌，周三两点一刻打网球，周四五点十分健身。你呢？

不但…，而且 ěrqiě…/ not only…, but also…；选 xuǎn / to choose；
需要 xūyào / to need；送 sòng / to give someone a ride；常 cháng / often；
差不多 / almost；除了 chúle / besides；活动 huódòng / activity；

Culture Focus

Many Chinese holidays are based on lunar dates. Name all the Chinese public holidays, and find out the dates of three major Chinese holidays of 2017.

shàng yī　máo yī　bèi xīn er
上 衣，毛 衣，背 心 儿，

xù shān　chèn shān　bèi xīn er
T-恤衫，衬 衫，背 心 儿，

dà yī　nèi yī　bèi xīn er
大衣，内衣，背 心 儿，

yùn dòng shān　hàn shān　bèi xīn er
运 动 衫，汗 衫，背 心 儿。

cháng kù　duǎn kù　bèi xīn er
长 裤，短 裤，背 心 儿，

chèn kù　nèi kù　bèi xīn er
衬 裤，内 裤，背 心 儿，

niú zǎi kù　máo kù　bèi xīn er
牛 仔 裤，毛 裤，背 心 儿，

kù zi　kù chǎ　bèi xīn er
裤子，裤 衩，背 心 儿。

cháng qún　duǎn qún　bèi xīn er
长 裙，短 裙，背 心 儿，

chèn qún　bù qún　bèi xīn er
衬 裙，布 裙，背 心 儿，

niú zǎi qún　mí nǐ qún　bèi xīn er
牛 仔 裙，迷 你 裙，背 心 儿，

lián yī qún　tào qún　bèi xīn er
连 衣 裙，套 裙，背 心 儿。

yī fu　kù zi　bèi xīn er
衣 服，裤 子，背 心 儿，

qún zi　shuì yī　bèi xīn er
裙 子，睡 衣，背 心 儿，

mào zi　xié wà　bèi xīn er
帽 子，鞋 袜，背 心 儿，

rén rén dōu yǒu bèi xīn er
人 人 都 有 背 心 儿！

Key words

1	背心儿	bèixīnr	vest
2	上衣	shàngyī	coat
3	毛衣	máoyī	sweater
4	T-恤衫	T-xùshān	T-shirt
5	衬衫	chènshān	shirt
6	大衣	dàyī	overcoat
7	内衣	nèiyī	undershirt
8	汗衫	hànshān	undershirt
9	裤子	kùzi	pants
10	衬裤	chènkù	underpants
11	内裤	nèikù	underwear
12	牛仔裤	niúzǎikù	jeans
13	迷你裙	mínǐqún	miniskirt
14	连衣裙	liányīqún	dress
15	套裙	tàoqún	dress suit
16	衣服	yīfu	clothes
17	帽子	màozi	hat
18	鞋	xié	shoes
19	袜子	wàzi	socks

Let the words flow!

We frequently leave our house in the morning in a hurry. However, making a few minor changes in our routine will be helpful. Try making some preparation the night before.

kuài diǎn er ba   bā diǎn le   zài bù qǐ lái jiù wǎn le
快 点 儿 吧，八 点 了！再 不 起 来 就 晚 了。

xǐ xǐ liǎn   shuā shuā yá   chī gè jiān dàn   hē bēi chá
洗 洗 脸，刷 刷 牙，吃 个 煎 蛋，喝 杯 茶。

bù rán shàng xué yòu huì wǎn   lǎo shī yòu yào mà nǐ lǎn
不 然 上 学 又 会 晚，老 师 又 要 骂 你 懒。

mā ma   mā ma   bié zháo jí
妈 妈，妈 妈，别 着 急。

hái yǒu qī fēn zhōng   jué duì lái de jí
还 有 七 分 钟，绝 对 来 得 及。

wǒ yòng yì fēn zhōng xǐ zǎo   yì fēn zhōng chuān yī
我 用 一 分 钟 洗 澡，一 分 钟 穿 衣，

yì fēn zhōng chuān xié wà   yì fēn zhōng chī jī
一 分 钟 穿 鞋 袜，一 分 钟 吃 鸡。

shèng xià sān fēn zhōng   wǒ pǎo dào xué xiào qù
剩 下 三 分 钟，我 跑 到 学 校 去。

zāo gāo   zhēn zāo gāo
糟 糕！真 糟 糕！

wǒ wàng le dài shū bāo
我 忘 了 带 书 包！

Key words

1	担心	dānxīn	to worry; anxious;
2	点儿	diǎnr	a little bit
3	洗脸	xǐ liǎn	to wash face
4	刷牙	shuā yá	to brush teeth
5	煎蛋	jiāndàn	fried egg
6	不然	bùrán	otherwise
7	又	yòu	once again
8	骂	mà	to scold
9	懒	lǎn	lazy
10	着急	zháojí	to feel anxious; to worry
11	分钟	fēngzhōng	minute
12	绝对	juéduì	absolutely
13	来得及	láidejí	There is still time for….
14	洗澡	xǐzǎo	to take a shower or bath
15	穿	chuān	to wear; to put on (clothes)
16	剩下	shèngxià	to remain; left over
17	到	dào	to (a place); until (a time); to arrive to
18	糟糕	zāogāo	Too bad! How terrible!
19	忘	wàng	to forget

Language Focus

3.1 Vocabulary Review.

Read it aloud. Translate it into English.
Write it in Chinese characters, and say it aloud again as you write it.

	English	**Chinese**
1. 快点儿起床吧!	_____	_____
2. 早睡早起	_____	_____
3. 好好洗脸	_____	_____
4. 吃两个煎蛋	_____	_____
5. 不然	_____	_____
6. 马骂妈妈懒。	_____	_____
7. 你又来晚了!	_____	_____
8. 着什么急?	_____	_____
9. 剩下的时间	_____	_____
10. 别忘了刷牙。	_____	_____
11. 穿好衣服再走。	_____	_____
12. 绝对来得及!	_____	_____
13. 别告诉咱妈。	_____	_____
14. 该洗澡啦!	_____	_____

 Whether it's the beginning of the school year, the middle, or the end, it is never too late to make a fresh start. From organizing your study space at home or getting school supplies, a few simple preparations will help you a lot.

3.2 Measure Words Review.

Please use an online dictionary to look up the words you don't know, or ask your teacher.

Use a color when describe each picture.

红，绿，黄，蓝，黑，白，灰，粉，紫，棕，金，银，橙，深，浅，

1 一条白短裤

2 ___

3 ___

4 ___

5 ___

6 ___

7 ___

8 ___

9 ___

10 ___

11 ___

12 ___

13 ___

14 ___

15 ___

16 ___

1. 学生该不该穿校服上学？ _____

2. 你什么颜色的衣服多？ _____

3.3 Grammar: The verbs 穿 & 戴.

> 穿 chuān: to wear or to put on clothes, shoes, socks…
>
> 戴 dài: to wear or to put on a hat, glasses, gloves, tie, jewelry (accessories)…

Use 穿 or 戴？

Please write down the complete phrases.

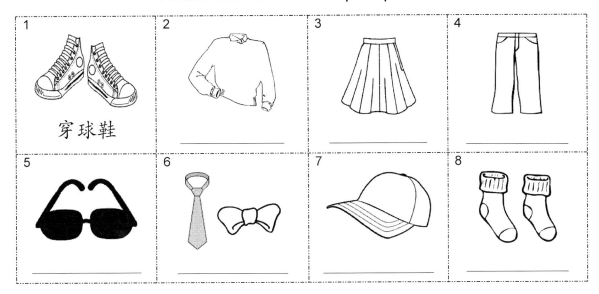

1 穿球鞋	2	3	4
5	6	7	8

3.4 Clothes for Every Season

Write the names of clothes under the season they are worn.
You can place some clothes in more than one season.

> 大衣，长裤，短裤，裙子，T-恤衫，背心儿，睡衣，球鞋，雨衣，
> 裤裙，短裙，牛仔裤，衬衫，内裤，袜子，毛衣，连衣裙，汗衫，

春天	夏天	秋天	冬天

3.5 Grammar: The sequence words

Sequence words are words that help us understand the order of events that are happening in the story.

先 xiān / first
先刷牙后洗脸。
Brush your teeth first, and then wash your face.

然后 ránhòu / then
你先做作业，然后再看电视！
Do your homework first, and then watch TV.

再 zài / again
吃了饭再玩。
Play after the meal.

最后 zuìhòu / finally
我先吃晚饭，然后看电视，

最后才写我的历史报告。
I ate my dinner first, then watched TV, and finally wrote my history report.

Now use the above words to describe the sequence of the pictures.
Use your imagination. Say as much as you can.

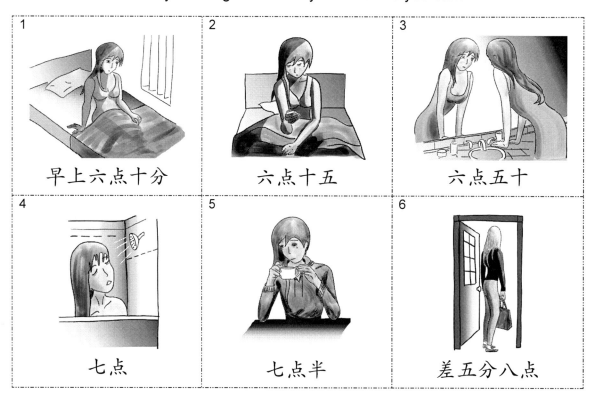

| 1 早上六点十分 | 2 六点十五 | 3 六点五十 |
| 4 七点 | 5 七点半 | 6 差五分八点 |

3.6 Grammar: The adverbs 又，再，还

又 is used to express an action or an event that has already happened.

你昨天来晚了，今天怎么又来晚了?!

You were late yesterday, how come you are late again today?!

再 is used to express an action or an event that is about to happen again.

如果你明天再来晚，你就别进教室了。

If you are late again tomorrow, don't enter the classroom.

还 is used to express an action or an event that has started.

你怎么还在睡觉?

How come you are still sleeping?!

1. Please don't be late again.

_____

2. Why do you want to read this novel again? It's too boring.

_____

3. Sorry, I forgot to bring money again.

_____

4. It's still raining. Let's go home and watch "外星人".

_____

5. Give him a call. Let him know we are still waiting for him.

_____

6. I want to visit China again, because I miss my friends there.

 Write down all your homework assignments. Then number them in the order that you plan to do them. Hint: Get the hardest work done first.

3.7 Grammar Review: The resultative complements

Unlike English, verbs in Chinese do not indicate the result of actions. When you want to indicate the result of an action, a resultative complement is placed after an action verb. Please remember only stative verbs and verbs can be used as resultative complements.

Here are some stative verbs or verbs used as resultive complements.

好	properly; in a proper way 坐好，拿好，吃好，写好，想好	上课了，请大家坐好。
会	to master a skill 学会，	我学会了开车。
见	to have seen; heard 听见，看见	我听见有人说话。
到	1）to have done something successfully, 　找到，买到，收到 2）to reach a place, a time, a level 　看到，学到，走到，听到，做到	我找到了书包。 我们学到了第三课。
完	to finish 看完，吃完，做完，写完，说完	做完作业再玩儿吧。

Fill in the blanks with the proper word given.

1. 警察还没有找_____我的狗。　　　　　　(会，到，完)

2. 我妹妹学_____了游泳。　　　　　　　　(见，到，会)

3. 我妈要我穿_____衣服再出去。　　　　　(好，见，完)

4. 下课啦，可我还没做_____考题。　　　　(到，完，会)

5. 我没听_____他在说什么。　　　　　　　(会，见，完)

6. 八点半，大明跑_____学校去了。　　　　(完，会，到)

7. 请想_____了再说。　　　　　　　　　　(完，好，会)

3.8 What time do you do these things?

Use the following words to talk about your daily routines.

Time frequency:	常，常常，不常，很少，
Sequence words:	先...，然后...，再...，最后...。
Activities:	起床，洗澡，吃早饭，坐校车，上学，上课， 吃午饭，放学以后，做运动，回家，做作业， 吃晚饭，看电视，听歌，看书，睡觉，

3.9 Good habits or bad habits?

	习惯 xíguàn / Habits	好不好？
1	我喜欢早睡早起。	
2	我喜欢晚睡晚起，早饭和中饭一起吃。	
3	我不在家做作业，只在学校做。	
4	我常做完作业才上网。	
5	我爱吃肉，不爱吃菜。	
6	我常喝水和果汁。	
7	我在学校只喝可乐，七喜和芬达。	
8	我起床晚，来不及吃早饭。	
9	吃饭前我会洗手。	
10	我一个星期刷三次牙。	
11	上汉语课我常坐在教室后面画画儿。	
12	我每天骑车上学。	
13	我很少吃糖。	
14	我每天上网跟朋友玩三个小时的游戏。	
15	我每天都半夜睡觉。	
16	周末我会睡到下午一点。	
17	我每天都会看两个小时的小说。	
18	我想吃就吃，想喝就喝，想玩就玩。	

Nearly everything we do in life is the result of our habits.

3.10 Reading & Speaking

快七点半啦，丽丽还在床上，她想再睡一会儿。丽丽**觉得**很累，因为她昨晚快十二点了才睡觉。昨天晚上她做了一个半小时的作业，看了两个多小时的电视。十一点她又上网玩了半个小时的**游戏**。**要不是**妈妈让她早点儿睡，她可能一晚上都不睡。丽丽总是晚上不想睡早上起不来。她每天早上都说：怎么又七点啦?!

已经七点三刻了，丽丽知道她今天上学又要晚了。如果她现在就去学校，她不会晚。可是，她现在还在床上呢。丽丽**得**洗澡，因为她**已经**两天没洗澡了。她得穿衣服。她得吃两个煎蛋。她得喝一杯牛奶。她得刷牙。她得找她的东西：书包，电脑，手机什么的。她还得跟爸妈说再见。

丽丽知道她今天又晚了，所以就慢慢地洗澡，慢慢地穿衣服，慢慢地吃早饭，慢慢地喝牛奶和果汁，慢慢地刷牙，慢慢地找书包，电脑，手机什么的。丽丽去跟爸妈再见。爸妈见到她说：小丽，这么早就起来啦! 今天是周六。

觉得 juéde / to feel; 要不是 / if not; 游戏 yóuxì / game;

得 děi / to have to; 已经 yǐjīng / already;

3.11 word detective — Not so new

Here are some basic Chinese characters you have learned.
Let's see if you can decode their meanings.

	Pinyin	English	Make a sentence
1. 剩饭	_____	_____	_____
2. 说唱乐	_____	_____	_____
3. 懒蛋	_____	_____	_____

3.12 Every picture tells a story- - What's yours?

Use your imagination. Write as much as you can.

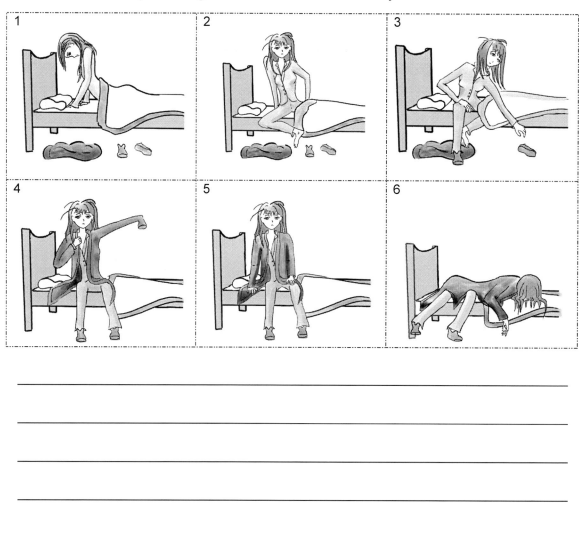

_____

_____

_____

_____

_____

3.13 Fun with Chinese radicals

A Chinese character often represents a part of history, an image, an idea, or an attitude about life.

For example, the character for blind is 盲. It consists of two parts: 亡 (to die, dead) and 目 (eye). A dead eye means a blind eye.

Just like the Lego bricks you use to build with, the Chinese radicals or commonly used Chinese characters are blocks that can be combined with each other to make new words.

衤	Write down the characters with 衤 in it.
衤 is related to clothes, and is always placed on the left side.	
刂	Write down the characters with 刂 in it.
刂 is related to knife, and is always placed on the right side of a Chinese character.	

Culture Focus

In many societies, norms about clothing reflect standards of modesty, religion, gender, and social status. Clothing may also function as a form of adornment and an expression of personal taste or style.

1. 旗袍
qípáo

2. 唐装
tángzhuāng

3. 中山装
zhōngshānzhuāng

The official currency in China is called Rénmínbì, which means " the people's money".

The Rénmínbì are 元 (yuán), 角 (jiǎo), and 分 (fēn).　　1 yuán = 10 jiǎo = 100 fēn.

yì fēn qián　　liǎng fēn qián
一 分 钱 ， 两 分 钱 ，

sān fēn　　sì fēn　　wǔ fēn qián
三 分 ， 四 分 ， 五 分 钱 。

yì máo qián　　liǎng máo qián
一 毛 钱 ， 两 毛 钱 ，

sān máo　　sì máo　　wǔ máo qián
三 毛 ， 四 毛 ， 五 毛 钱 。

yí kuài qián　　liǎng kuài qián
一 块 钱 ， 两 块 钱 ，

sān kuài　　sì kuài　　wǔ kuài qián
三 块 ， 四 块 ， 五 块 钱 。

yì bǎi kuài　　liǎng bǎi kuài
一 百 块 ， 两 百 块 ，

sān bǎi　　sì bǎi　　wǔ bǎi kuài
三 百 ， 四 百 ， 五 百 块 。

yì qiān kuài　　liǎng qiān kuài
一 千 块 ， 两 千 块 ，

sān qiān　　sì qiān　　wǔ qiān kuài
三 千 ， 四 千 ， 五 千 块 。

yí wàn kuài　　liǎng wàn kuài
一 万 块 ， 两 万 块 ，

sān wàn　　sì wàn　　wǔ wàn kuài
三 万 ， 四 万 ， 五 万 块 。

yí kuài èr　　liǎng kuài sān
一 块 二 ， 两 块 三 ，

yì bǎi èr shí sān kuài qī máo sān
一 百 二 十 三 块 七 毛 三 。

Key words

1	钱	qián	money
2	多少钱？	duōshǎo qián	How much is it?
3	分	fēn	Chinese currency for penny
4	毛	máo	Chinese currency for ten cents
5	块	kuài	colloquial word for 元 yuán, a unit currency such as dollar
6	元	yuán	dollar
7	角	jiǎo	Chinese currency for ten cents
8	人民币	rénmínbì	official name of Chinese currency
9	港圆	gǎngyuán	Hong Kong Dollar
10	美元	měiyuán	American Dollar
11	加元	jiāyuán	Canadian Dollar
12	英镑	yīngbàng	Pound
13	欧元	ōuyuán	Euro
14	日圆	rìyuán	Japanese Dollar
15	银行	yínháng	bank
16	换钱	huàn qián	to exchange money

The Chinese currency is called Rénmínbì (people's currency) and is abbreviated as RMB. The symbol for the RMB is ¥. The basic unit is the yuán. Ten jiǎo make one yuán; ten fēn equal one jiǎo. Chinese currency consists of paper notes and hard coins.

Let the words flow!

There's a saying "Everything in China is negotiable." You can bargain for most things in China. Don't feel bad or shy about negotiating.

zá zhì duō shǎo qián
杂 志 多 少 钱?

qī kuài liù máo sān
七 块 六 毛 三。

shǒu biǎo duō shǎo qián
手 表 多 少 钱?

bā bǎi jiǔ shí sān
八 百 九 十 三。

zěn me nà me guì
怎 么 那 么 贵?

néng bu néng pián yi diǎn er
能 不 能 便 宜 点 儿?

nǐ xiǎng gěi duō shǎo
你 想 给 多 少?

yì bǎi èr shí sān
一 百 二 十 三。

liù bǎi wǔ shí sān
六 百 五 十 三。

yì bǎi èr shí sān
一 百 二 十 三。

sì bǎi wǔ shí sān
四 百 五 十 三。

tài guì le   bú yào
太 贵 了! 不 要!

bié zǒu   bié zǒu
别 走! 别 走!

yì bǎi èr shí sān gěi nǐ la
一 百 二 十 三 给 你 啦!

zhè lǎo wài   tǐng huì kǎn jià
这 老 外, 挺 会 砍 价!

Key words

1	杂志	zázhì	magazine
2	手表	shǒubiǎo	wrist watch
3	怎么	zěnme	How come...?
4	那么	nàme	so much; that much; in that case
5	贵	guì	expensive; noble
6	能	néng	to be able to
7	便宜	piányì	cheap; inexpensive
8	老外	lǎowài	foreigner (nickname for foreigners)
9	会	huì	to know how; can; likely
10	砍价	kǎnjià	to bargain
11	刷卡	shuākǎ	to use a credit card
12	现金	xiànjīn	cash
13	挣钱	zhèngqián	to earn money
14	花钱	huāqián	to spend money
15	时髦	shímáo	fashionable
16	名牌	míngpái	famous brand
17	大号	dàhào	large size
18	中号	zhōnghào	medium size
19	小号	xiǎohào	small size

Language Focus

4.1 Vocabulary Review.

Read it aloud. Translate it into English.
Write it in Chinese characters, and say it aloud again as you write it.

	English	**Chinese**
1. 便宜点儿吧!	_____	_____
2. 怎么这么贵?!	_____	_____
3. 墨镜多少钱?	_____	_____
4. 我只有十五块。	_____	_____
5. 真会砍价!	_____	_____
6. 五万三	_____	_____
7. 两块钱一本。	_____	_____
8. 动物杂志	_____	_____
9. 表慢了两分钟。	_____	_____
10. 少花钱吧!	_____	_____
11. 你先拿去用。	_____	_____
12. 多少钱一件?	_____	_____
13. 不买别砍价!	_____	_____
14. 有中号的没有?	_____	_____

 De-junking will help you unclutter your brain. Clean out your backpack, old folders, and desk drawers. Trash stuff that no longer works or serve a purpose, like dried-up pens, worn-out erasers, or candy wrappers.

4.2 你喜欢哪个名牌？

	名牌	英文	国家	产品
1	阿迪达斯 ādídásī			
2	耐克 nàikè			
3	锐步 ruìbù			
4	彪马 piāomǎ			
5	斐乐 fěilè			
6	李宁 Lǐ Níng			
7	安踏 āntà			

1. 你喜欢什么名牌？ ＿＿＿＿＿＿＿＿＿＿＿＿

2. 人们为什么喜爱名牌？ ＿＿＿＿＿＿＿＿＿＿＿＿

3. 你的零用钱是哪儿来的？ ＿＿＿＿＿＿＿＿＿＿＿＿

4.3 钱包里有钱，还会有什么？

4.4 Stores in Town.

Imagine you're walking down a city street…

1 书店	2 冰淇淋店	3 电脑店
4 吉他店		5 宠物店
6 花店	7 饭店	8 咖啡店
9 衣帽店	10 Add your own	11 Add your own

1. 你喜欢去哪些商店？　_____

2. 你常和谁一起去？　_____

3. 如果你有一百块，你会买什么？　_____

4.5 Asking about the Price.

Shopping, buying and selling are games in China. The seller plays and the buyer plays. In the tourist-trade, everyone's out to make a deal, so you just have to learn the rules. Nothing opens the door for you like 多少钱？ 怎么卖？

Pretend to walk away. Generally, this skill works quite well in most shopping places. If the price proposed by the seller is still unacceptable, you should use the walk-away technique. Usually, you will be called back again, and the price you offered may be accepted.

Paying with small change is preferred. Do not show large denominations. Otherwise, the seller may hike the price when he discovers that you can afford the price he asks.

请问，字典怎么卖？

太贵了！便宜点儿吧！

二十怎么样？

九十九块一本。

五十拿去吧。

不卖！

Work in Pairs.

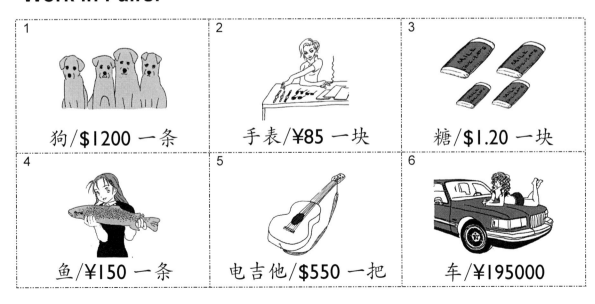

1 狗/$1200 一条	2 手表/¥85 一块	3 糖/$1.20 一块
4 鱼/¥150 一条	5 电吉他/$550 一把	6 车/¥195000

4.6   Jobs for Teens.

Believe it or not, there are many jobs you can find.

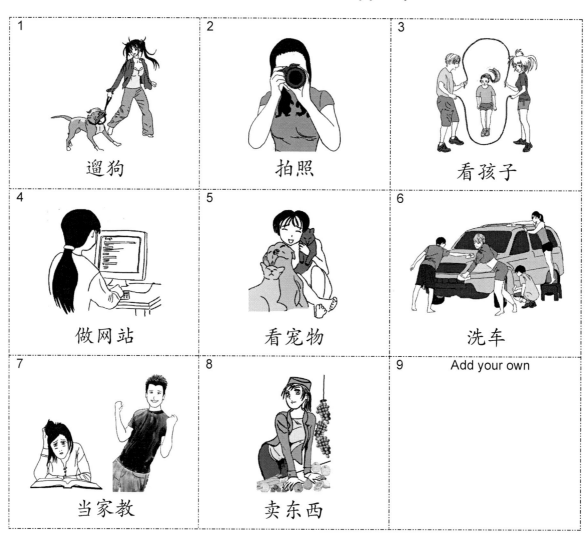

1 遛狗	2 拍照	3 看孩子
4 做网站	5 看宠物	6 洗车
7 当家教	8 卖东西	9 Add your own

Work in pairs.

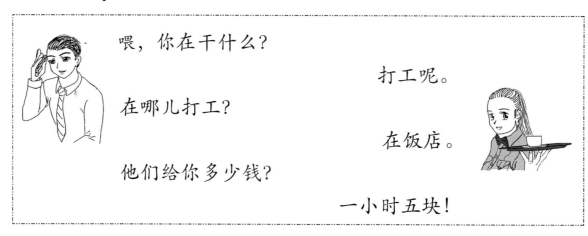

喂，你在干什么？

打工呢。

在哪儿打工？

在饭店。

他们给你多少钱？

一小时五块！

4.7 Work in pairs.

China is a fantastic shopping destination. From clothes to music CDs, you're bound to be able to buy it in China.   When shopping in China, please keep one thing in mind. That is everything in China is negotiable.

小姐想买什么？

这本怎么样？

这两本你看看。

三十二块。

你想给多少？

拿去吧！

有**汉英字典**吗？
不要太大的。

这是小学生字典，
    小了点儿。

这本不错，多少钱？

三十二块？
太贵了吧！

十五块。
我只有十五块。

Now you can use the above dialogue as an example to make your own.

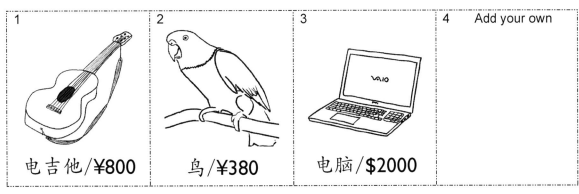

1	2	3	4 Add your own
电吉他/¥800	鸟/¥380	电脑/$2000	

4.8 On the Same Team

The words on this team all have something in common, except for one. Can you find that one word that doesn't? Write it down at the end of the line.

1. 球鞋，雨鞋，凉鞋，跑鞋，买鞋 　　　　　　＿＿＿＿＿＿

2. 上衣，背心儿，洗衣服，毛衣，衬衫 　　　　＿＿＿＿＿＿

3. 男警察，律师，电工，橡皮，画家 　　　　　＿＿＿＿＿＿

4. 红，黄，茶，蓝，绿，黑，粉，紫 　　　　　＿＿＿＿＿＿

5. 直，长，当，多，卷，美，好看 　　　　　　＿＿＿＿＿＿

6. 冰茶，果汁，巧克力，七喜，芬达 　　　　　＿＿＿＿＿＿

7. 鸭，狗，熊猫，羊，护士，奶牛 　　　　　　＿＿＿＿＿＿

8. 睡觉，游泳，吃饭，喝水，有名 　　　　　　＿＿＿＿＿＿

9. 滑雪，溜冰，骑车，烤鸭，冲浪 　　　　　　＿＿＿＿＿＿

10. 请，下，里，外，前，后，上，左 　　　　　＿＿＿＿＿＿

11. 学校，学生，同学，老师，上学 　　　　　　＿＿＿＿＿＿

12. 很，非常，太，和，也，真 　　　　　　　　＿＿＿＿＿＿

13. 新年，春节，季节，圣诞节，情人节 　　　　＿＿＿＿＿＿

14. 日本，德国，意大利，伦敦，新西兰 　　　　＿＿＿＿＿＿

15. 眉毛，嘴，肚子，眼镜，胳膊，右脚 　　　　＿＿＿＿＿＿

16. 少，慢，快，热，累，给，早，忙 　　　　　＿＿＿＿＿＿

17. 人民币，便宜，日圆，美元，欧元 　　　　　＿＿＿＿＿＿

4.9 Survey the Class

Walk around the class and talk to your classmates. Compliment them on something they have. And then ask them questions.

姓名	东西	价钱	商店
同学 1			
同学 2			
同学 3			

4.10 穿衣戴帽

1	在你的学校，学生不可以穿什么上学？
2	设计 (shèjì, to design) 一件 T-恤衫。 What's the message on it? 看谁的设计最受欢迎。

艾米喜欢逛商店。她什么商店都爱逛：衣服店，鞋帽店，书店，电脑店，墨镜店，糖店，花店，吉他店，茶店，宠物店什么的。明天是星期六，艾米想去鞋店买一双鞋。她想买一双红色的皮鞋。艾米什么颜色的鞋都有，可是她没有红皮鞋。艾米觉得红色的皮鞋好看，她觉得她该有一双红皮鞋。

艾米什么颜色的衣服都有：白色的长裙，黑色的裤子，绿色的衬衫，粉色的毛衣，浅蓝色的牛仔裙，深紫色的运动衫。艾米觉得她的白裙子可以和红皮鞋一起穿，她的黑裤子也可以和红皮鞋一起穿。下周末学校有舞会，艾米打算穿白色长裙和红皮鞋去跳舞。可是，穿什么衬衫呢？穿红皮鞋不能穿绿衬衫，因为红色跟绿色一起穿难看死了。穿红皮鞋也不能穿粉毛衣，因为红色和粉色一起穿也难看死了。想来想去艾米觉得还该买一件衬衫。买什么颜色的衬衫呢？想来想去，艾米决定买一件黑衬衫，因为黑衬衫配什么都可以。

艾米很高兴明天是周六，因为她又可以去逛商店了。想着想着，艾米睡着了。

逛 guàng / to stroll; 皮鞋 píxié / leather shoes; 打算 dǎsuàn / to plan
舞会 wǔhuì / dance party; 决定 juédìng / to decide; 配 pèi / to match

4.12   Every picture tells a story- - What's yours?

Look at the picture below. Make sure to notice all the details.
Then use your imagination to write a story about them.

你看见什么了?	你听见什么了?

你 的 故 事

_____

_____

_____

_____

_____

_____

4.13 Fun with Chinese radicals

 A Chinese character often represents a part of history, an image, an idea, or an attitude about life.

For example, the character for treasure is 宝. It consists of two parts: 宀 (roof/house) and 玉 (jade). Treasures hide in a house.

人	Write down the characters with 人 in it.
人 is related to person, and its position is on the top.	
灬	Write down the characters with 灬 in it.
灬 is related to fire, and is usually placed on the bottom.	

4.14 word detective Not so new

Here are some basic Chinese characters you have learned.
Let's see if you can decode their meanings.

	Pinyin	English	Make a sentence
1. 分手	_____	_____	_____
2. 贵客	_____	_____	_____
3. 别的	_____	_____	_____

Culture Focus

1. China has many significant inventions. Please list six great inventions.

_____

_____

Chinese adjectives differ from their English counterparts. Although Chinese adjectives have functions to modify nouns like English adjectives, they also function as verbs when used as predicates. This rhyme teaches you some common Chinese adjectives. So, clap your hands or tap your toe or stamp your feet while rhyming it! You will be surprised how easy it is to learn them.

yí gè dà   yí gè xiǎo   yì tóu xiàng   yì zhī niǎo
一个大，一个小：一头象，一只鸟。

yí gè duō   yí gè shǎo   yì bǎ mǐ   yí gè zǎo
一个多，一个少：一把米，一个枣。

yí gè gāo   yí gè ǎi   yí zuò shān   yì bēi nǎi
一个高，一个矮：一座山，一杯奶。

yí gè pàng   yí gè shòu   yì tóu zhū   yí kuài ròu
一个胖，一个瘦：一头猪，一块肉。

yí gè zhòng   yí gè qīng   yì tǒng shuǐ   yì zhǎn dēng
一个重，一个轻：一桶水，一盏灯。

yí gè kuài   yí gè màn   yí liàng chē   yì wǎn fàn
一个快，一个慢：一辆车，一碗饭。

yí gè cháng   yí gè duǎn   yì tiáo shéng   yì bǎ sǎn
一个长，一个短：一条绳，一把伞。

yí gè rè   yí gè lěng   yì hú chá   yì zhāng bǐng
一个热，一个冷：一壶茶，一张饼。

yí gè xiāng   yí gè chòu   yì pán cài   yì bǎ dòu
一个香，一个臭：一盘菜，一把豆。

zhèi gè shēn   nà gè qiǎn   zhèi gè róng yì   nà gè nán
这个深，那个浅。这个容易，那个难。

zhèi gè suān   nà gè tián   zhèi gè qīng dàn   nà gè xián
这个酸，那个甜。这个清淡，那个咸。

Key words

1	高	gāo	tall; high
2	矮	ǎi	short (vertically short)
3	胖	pàng	fat; over-weight
4	瘦	shòu	skinny; thin
5	重	zhòng	heavy
6	轻	qīng	light weight
7	香	xiāng	fragrant
8	臭	chòu	smelly; stink
9	绳	shéng	rope
10	伞	sǎn	umbrella
11	冷	lěng	cold
12	深	shēn	deep (water, a hole); dark (color)
13	浅	qiǎn	shallow (water, a hole); light (color)
14	容易	róngyì	easy
15	难	nán	difficult; hard
16	酸	suān	sour
17	甜	tián	sweet
18	清淡	qīngdàn	light (taste of food); not greasy
19	咸	xián	salty

Let the words flow!

Examine objects to ascertain how they are different, and then organize your thoughts before describing them.

nǐ duō dà　　tā duō dà
你多大？她多大？

nǐ liǎ shì bú shì yí yàng dà
你俩是不是一样大？

wǒ shí qī　　tā shí bā
我十七，她十八。

wǒ bǐ tā xiǎo　　tā bǐ wǒ dà
我比她小，她比我大。

nǐ duō dà　　tā duō dà
你多大？她多大？

nǐ liǎ shì bú shì yí yàng dà
你俩是不是一样大？

wǒ shí qī　　tā shí bā
我十七，她十八。

wǒ méi tā gāo　　yě méi tā dà
我没她高，也没她大。

nǐ duō dà　　tā duō dà
你多大？他多大？

nǐ liǎ shì bú shì yí yàng dà
你俩是不是一样大？

wǒ liǎ jīn nián dōu shí bā
我俩今年都十八。

wǒ men gē liǎ yí yàng dà
我们哥俩一样大。

Key words

1	多…	duō	How + adjectives?
2	多大	duō dà	How old? (for age older than 10)
3	俩	liǎ	two people
4	一样	yíyàng	same
5	比	bǐ	to compare
6	哥俩	gēliǎ	brothers
7	姐俩	jiěliǎ	sisters
8	更	gèng	more; even more (before an adj. or a verb)
9	最	zuì	the most; --est (before an adj. or a verb)
10	穷	qióng	poor
11	富	fù	rich; wealthy
12	聪明	cōngmíng	smart
13	笨	bèn	stupid
14	随和	suíhé	easy-going
15	挑剔	tiāotì	picky
16	帅	shuài	handsome
17	丑	chǒu	ugly
18	内向	nèixiàng	introverted
19	外向	wàixiàng	extroverted

Language Focus

5.1 Vocabulary Review.

Read it aloud. Translate it into English.
Write it in Chinese characters, and say it aloud again as you write it.

	English	**Chinese**
1. 高矮不同	_____	_____
2. 瘦猫挺爱玩儿。	_____	_____
3. 深蓝色的毛衣	_____	_____
4. 你今年多大?	_____	_____
5. 我俩不一样高。	_____	_____
6. 数学题很容易。	_____	_____
7. 饭菜都太咸了!	_____	_____
8. 吃清淡点儿好。	_____	_____
9. 我没那么胖吧。	_____	_____
10. 真难看!	_____	_____
11. 有深有浅	_____	_____
12. 大大小小	_____	_____
13. 咱姐俩好说。	_____	_____
14. 聪明的孩子	_____	_____

 Adjectives are words we use to describe people, places or things. They tell us what kind, or how many, or which particular one we are talking about. In Chinese, an adjective is always placed before whatever it describes.

5.2 Adjective Review.

Use an adjective to describe each picture. Write the phrases.
Use a proper measure word, when needed.

大，小，多，少，长，短，直，卷，高，矮，胖，肥，瘦，

新，旧，老，少，轻，重，快，慢，香，臭，深，浅，容易，

难，甜，酸，辣，咸，清淡，好看，高兴，累，忙，贵，便宜

5.3 The use of 比

比 is used to compare objects or actions.

Positive:　　A 比 B ＋ adjective

我比我朋友高。
I am taller than my friend.

Negative:　　A 不比 B ＋ Adjective　　or　　A 没 B ＋ Adjective

我不比我朋友高。　　　　我没我朋友高。
I am not taller than my friend.　　I am not taller than my friend.

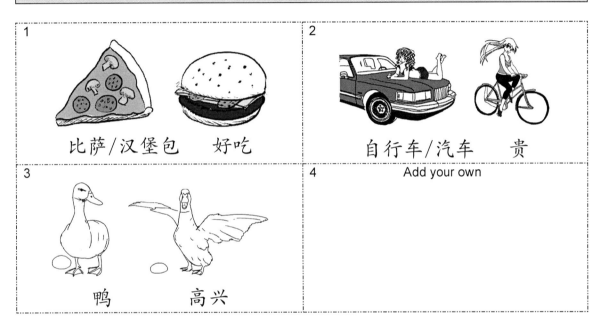

1	2
比萨/汉堡包　　好吃	自行车/汽车　　贵
3	4　Add your own
鸭　　高兴	

1. _____positive

   _____negative

2. _____positive

   _____negative

3. _____positive

   _____negative

4. _____positive

   _____negative

5.4 The use of 跟....一样

跟...一样 (same as) is used to show that two objects or two actions are the same.

Positive: A 跟 B 一样 + adjective

我跟我朋友一样高。
I am as tall as my friend.

Negative: A 跟 B 不一样 + adjective

我跟我朋友不一样高。
I am not as tall as my friend.

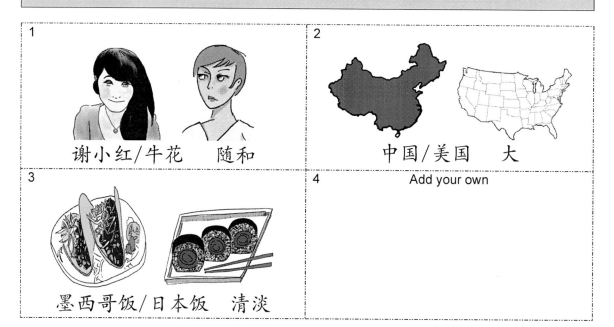

1	2
谢小红/牛花　随和	中国/美国　大
3	4 Add your own
墨西哥饭/日本饭　清淡	

1. _____ positive

   _____ negative

2. _____ positive

   _____ negative

3. _____ positive

   _____ negative

4. _____ positive

   _____ negative

5.5 The use of 更 & 最

更 gèng / even: 更 is used to express that A is even more so than B.

我比我朋友更高。

I am even taller than my friend.

最 zuì / the most: 最 is used to express the highest degree of quality or quantity.

我们班我最高。

In our class, I am the tallest.

Just like English, 很，真，太，非常 are not used in 比 sentences.

Instead 得多，多了 are used after the adjective.

我比我朋友高得多。　　　我比我朋友高多了。

I am much taller than my friend.　　I am much taller than my friend.

1	2
 谁最不高兴?	 哪个国家更大?
3  哪个最好吃?	4　　　　Add your own

1. _____positive

   _____negative

3. _____positive

   _____negative

5.6 Work in Pairs.

你说我该学什么？

汉语还是法语？

学汉语。

为什么？

因为汉语比法语<u>有用</u>。

好，听你的。

Now you can use the above dialogue as an example to make your own.

1 开车还是骑车？

2 养狗还是养鸟？

3 给她字典还是墨镜？

4 Add your own

5.7 Talk about it!

Choose one topic. Think about it, write about it, and share it with your classmates.

1. 两年后你多大？两年后的你跟现在的你会有什么不同？

2. 电子书好还是纸书好？为什么？

3. 你在朋友家吃饭跟在自己家吃饭有什么不一样？

我们不一样

我十六，我哥比我大两岁。谁都说我跟我哥不像哥俩：我的眼睛是咖啡色的，我哥的是蓝色的。我们俩都有黄头发，但是我的头发直，我哥的头发卷。我又高又瘦，我哥又矮又胖。我走得快，我哥走得慢。我喜欢穿深颜色的衣服，我哥喜欢穿浅颜色的衣服。我喜欢早睡早起，我哥喜欢晚睡晚起。我喜欢打棒球，我哥喜欢下棋。没错，我跟我哥长得太不一样啦。不过，**生活**中，我跟我哥是好朋友。

我跟我妹也不一样。我二十五岁，我妹比我小三岁。我当老师，我妹当警察。我喜欢吃甜，我妹喜欢吃酸。我喜欢喝咖啡，我妹喜欢喝绿茶。我喜欢吃墨西哥饭，我妹只喜欢吃面：牛肉面，鸡肉面，猪肉面，鱼肉面，炒面或汤面什么的。我喜欢穿裙子，我妹不穿裙子，只穿牛仔裤。我喜欢看书，我妹喜欢听书。我有两条狗，我妹没有宠物。我开车上班，我妹骑车上班。周末我喜欢在家看电视。我妹家没电视，因为她觉得看电视没意思，她喜欢跟朋友去公园烧烤。我跟我妹长得像，可是因为我俩的**爱好**不同，朋友们都说我们不象姐俩。不过，生活中，我跟我妹是好朋友。

生活 shēnghuó / life;   爱好 àihào / hobby

Compare yourself with a member of your family, or one of your best friends.

5.9 Fun with Chinese radicals

Just like the Lego bricks you use to build almost anything, the Chinese radicals and commonly used Chinese characters are blocks that can be combined with each other to make endless new words.

A Chinese character often represents a part of history, an image, an idea, or an attitude about life.

For example, the character for to sit is 坐 . It consists of three parts: 土 (soil) and two 人 (person). It means two people sit on the ground talking.

It is said that every Chinese character contains a picture. So, use your imagination when studying Chinese characters. Have fun!

广	Write down the characters with 广 in it.
广 is related mostly to a space occupied. Its position is fixed.	
车 ➡ 车	Write down the characters with 车 in it.
车 is related to vehicles, and is always placed on the left side.	

5.10 word detective ~ Not so new

Here are some basic Chinese characters you have learned.
Let's see if you can decode their new meanings.

	Pinyin	English	Make a sentence
1. 高人	_____	_____	_____
2. 丑话	_____	_____	_____
3. 笨蛋	_____	_____	_____

5.11 Write a letter.

Your best friend is currently attending a different school. You would like to convince him or her to transfer to your school. Describe your school so that your friend will be interested in visiting or even transferring. You may want to describe the beautiful campus, the excellent faculty, the friendly students, the various sports and social activities.

Use your imagination. Write as many sentences as you can.

你来我的学校吧!

_____

_____

_____

_____

_____

_____

_____

_____

Culture Focus

Compare Beijing with Washington DC.

1. Similar: _____

2. Different: _____

The list can be long: in and out, up and down, above and under, behind and front, and so on. This chant will make learning the position words easy and fun.

shàng miàn   xià miàn   xià miàn   shàng miàn
上 面，下 面，下 面， 上 面。
shàng miàn de shū jià   shū jià shàng miàn
上 面 的 书 架，书 架 上 面。

zuǒ biān   yòu biān   yòu biān   zuǒ biān
左 边，右 边，右 边， 左 边。
zuǒ biān de wò shì   wò shì zuǒ biān
左 边 的 卧 室，卧 室 左 边。

qián miàn   hòu miàn   hòu miàn   qián miàn
前 面，后 面，后 面， 前 面。
qián miàn de fáng zi   fáng zi qián miàn
前 面 的 房 子，房 子 前 面。

lǐ miàn   wài miàn   wài miàn   lǐ miàn
里 面，外 面，外 面， 里 面。
lǐ miàn de fáng jiān   fáng jiān lǐ miàn
里 面 的 房 间，房 间 里 面。

páng biān   zhōng jiān   zhōng jiān   páng biān
旁 边，中 间，中 间， 旁 边。
páng biān de cè suǒ   cè suǒ páng biān
旁 边 的 厕 所，厕 所 旁 边。

duì miàn   duì miàn   duì miàn   duì miàn
对 面，对 面，对 面， 对 面。
duì miàn de gōng yuán   gōng yuán duì miàn
对 面 的 公 园，公 园 对 面。

Key words

1	上面	shàngmian	on top of
2	下面	xiàmian	below
3	书架	shūjià	bookshelf
4	左边	zuǒbiān	left; the left side; to the left side
5	右边	yòubiān	right; the right side; to the right side
6	前面	qiánmian	ahead; in front of
7	后面	hòumian	back; behind; rear
8	房子	fángzi	house
9	里面	lǐmian	inside
10	房间	fángjiān	room
11	外面	wàimian	outside
12	旁边	pángbiān	beside
13	中间	zhōngjiān	between; in the middle
14	对面	duìmian	opposite
15	公园	gōngyuán	park
16	阁楼	gélóu	attic
17	地下室	dìxiàshì	basement
18	洗手间	xǐshǒujiān	washroom; W.C
19	公寓	gōngyù	apartment

Let the words flow!

In Chinese, the words "before" and "after" are used slightly different than in English. In this rhyming dialogue, you will learn how to use them. Besides, you will also learn how to describe all the rooms in your house in Chinese.

yī diǎn yǐ qián nǐ gàn shá
一 点 以 前 你 干 啥?

wǒ zài fàn tīng hē bīng chá
我 在 饭 厅 喝 冰 茶。

liǎng diǎn yǐ qián nǐ gàn shá
两 点 以 前 你 干 啥?

wǒ zài chú fáng qiē xī guā
我 在 厨 房 切 西 瓜。

sān diǎn yǐ qián nǐ gàn shá
三 点 以 前 你 干 啥?

wǒ zài kè tīng liàn huà huà er
我 在 客 厅 练 画 画 儿。

sì diǎn yǐ qián nǐ gàn shá
四 点 以 前 你 干 啥?

wǒ zài wò shì xiě shēng rì kǎ
我 在 卧 室 写 生 日 卡。

wǔ diǎn yǐ qián nǐ gàn shá
五 点 以 前 你 干 啥?

wǒ zài bāng mā shōu shi jiā
我 在 帮 妈 收 拾 家。

nà me liù diǎn yǐ hòu ne
那 么, 六 点 以 后 呢?

wǒ xiān qù huā yuán wèi xiǎo tù
我 先 去 花 园 喂 小 兔,

rán hòu dǎ sǎo yù shì hé chē kù
然 后 打 扫 浴 室 和 车 库!

nǐ yě tài máng le
你 也 太 忙 了!

Key words

1	以前	yǐqián	before; formerly
2	以后	yǐhòu	after; later; afterwards
3	饭厅	fàntīng	dining-room
4	厨房	chúfáng	kitchen
5	切	qiē	to cut; to slice
6	客厅	kètīng	living-room
7	练	liàn	to practice
8	卧室	wòshì	bedroom
9	生日卡	shēngrìkǎ	birthday card
10	收拾	shōushi	to put (something) in order; to tidy up
11	先	xiān	first
12	花园	huāyuán	garden
13	兔	tù	rabbit
14	然后	ránhòu	and then; after that
15	打扫	dǎsǎo	to clean
16	浴室	yùshì	bathroom; shower-room
17	车库	chēkù	garage
18	得	děi	have to; must
19	整理	zhěnglǐ	to tidy up; to sort out

Language Focus

6.1 Vocabulary Review.

Read it aloud. Translate it into English.
Write it in Chinese characters, and say it aloud again as you write it.

	English	**Chinese**
1. 收拾收拾卧室	_____	_____
2. 打扫完客厅	_____	_____
3. 车库里的东西	_____	_____
4. 爸爸的书房	_____	_____
5. 对面的房子	_____	_____
6. 公园外面	_____	_____
7. 桌子上的杂志	_____	_____
8. 两个卧室中间	_____	_____
9. 厕所旁边	_____	_____
10. 下课以后呢?	_____	_____
11. 用完了给我用。	_____	_____
12. 上学以前	_____	_____
13. 写完信才睡觉	_____	_____
14. 我得回家了。	_____	_____

 What can you learn from playing sports? From growing plants? From having a pet? From being part of a family? From being a good friend? From taking care of a pet? From learning Chinese language?

6.2 Rooms & Activities.

他们在干什么？

如果你在这些地方的话，你会干什么？

1 客厅	2 卧室	3 教室
4 厨房	5 浴室	6 饭厅
7 商店	8 咖啡馆	9 书房
10 公园	11 Add your own	12 Add your own

6.3 Grammar: The use of 以前 & 以后

以前：before   a specific time ＋ 以前   or   an action ＋ 以前

我三点以前在学校。
I am at school before 3 o'clock.

吃饭前请洗手。
Wash your hands before eating.

以后：after   a specific time ＋ 以后   or   an action ＋ 以后

朋友们两点以后来我家。
Friends come to my house after 2:00pm.

下课以后咱们去游泳吧。
Let's swim after class.

1. Let's play basketball after 1:30pm today.

_____

2. I have to go to the pet store before going to your house.

_____

3. I will call you after finishing my homework.

_____

4. I told you I would clean my bedroom after dinner.

_____

5. Before studying Chinese, I thought it was difficult to learn.

_____

6. Brush your teeth before going to bed.

_____

6.4 Talk about it.

他们回家以前干什么了?

1 谢万_____

2 丽丽_____

3 王小红_____

4 艾米_____

5 石牛_____

6 李新_____

他们回家以后干什么了?

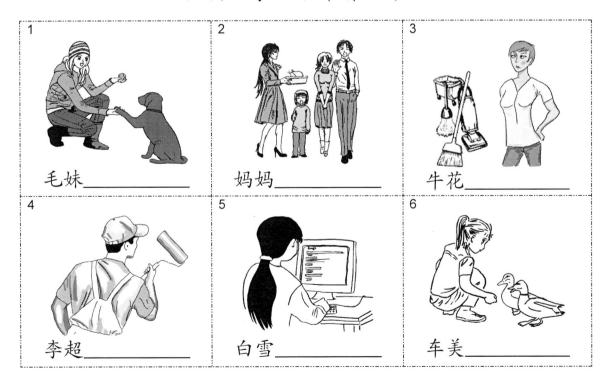

1 毛妹_____

2 妈妈_____

3 牛花_____

4 李超_____

5 白雪_____

6 车美_____

6.5 What is different?

这两家哪儿不一样？

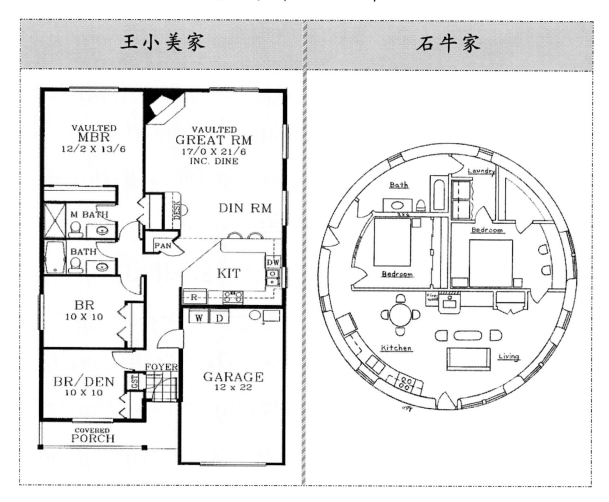

王小美家	石牛家

1. 客厅: _____

2. 饭厅: _____

3. 厨房: _____

4. 卧室: _____

5. 浴室: _____

6. 洗手间: _____

7. 车库: 王小美家有车库，在房子的前面。石牛家没车库。

6.6 想想看

高家有六个孩子：丽丽，同生，大明，小喜，万朋和红星。高家还有两条金毛狗，三只大胖猫，两只白鸭和五只鸡。因为高家人多，所以他们的房子很大，有七个卧室和四个浴室。高先生和高太太都有自己的书房。给你一分钟。一分钟以后请你说说高家的孩子在哪个卧室。

1. 万朋的卧室在同生的卧室上面。

2. 大明的卧室在丽丽和同生的卧室中间。

3. 丽丽的卧室在大树旁边。

4. 红星的卧室不在万朋的卧室旁边。

你要自己做。别看别人的，别问老师，也别问你旁边的同学。

6.7 The layout of your house.

Use your artistic skills to draw a map of your house for a visiting friend from China. Remember to add humor. Also, if you have a pet, indicate where it enjoys being.

1. 你家有几个卧室？ _____

2. 你卧室的对面有什么？ _____

3. 你的卧室里有电视没有？ _____

4. 你有自己的浴室吗？ _____

5. 谁打扫你的卧室？ _____

6. 你想一个人时会去哪儿？ _____

6.8 Grammar: The use of 有，是，在

有： noun + position word + 有 + noun.

学校前面有公园。

In front of the school is a park.

是： noun + position word + 是 + noun.

电脑旁边都是汉语书。

Chinese books are besides the computer.

在： noun + 在 + noun + position word.

汉语书在电脑旁边。

Chinese books are next to the computer.

Fill in the blanks with 是，有，在

1. 别找啦，你的墨镜_____桌子上。

2. 你的书包好重！里面_____什么？

3. 你们学校旁边_____公园吗？

4. 明星书店对面_____一家鞋店。

5. 高老师的教室_____电脑室的左边。

6. 厕所不_____书房旁边。

7. 书架上_____中文小说。

8. 车库里_____一辆红色跑车。

9. 两个房子的中间_____一棵大树。

10. 一只黑猫_____花园里。

6.9 Review: The location words

Identify 7 items in this drawing, and then tell us where the cats are.

猫在哪儿？

The items in this picture:

1. _____

2. _____

3. _____

4. _____

5. _____

6. _____

6.10 Fun with Chinese radicals

A Chinese character often represents a part of history, an image, an idea, or an attitude about life.

For example, the character for inferior is 劣. It consists of two parts: 少 (less) and 力 (strength).

厂	Write down the characters with 厂 in it.
厂 is related mostly to houses, and its position is fixed.	
户	Write down the characters with 户 in it.
户 is related mostly to door or household, and its position is fixed.	

6.11 word detective Not so new

Here are some basic Chinese characters you have learned.
Let's see if you can decode their meanings.

	Pinyin	English	Make a sentence
1. 外国	_____	_____	_____
2. 校园	_____	_____	_____
3. 公车	_____	_____	_____

Culture Focus

In the U.S the guest tries to respect the ways of the host. However, in China the guest is treated with great kindness and respect by the host and guests are encouraged to do what they like! Name a few proper manners when visiting a Chinese family.

Everyone has an opinion. Different opinions foster debate. And debate is great!

zhè jiàn shàng yī zěn me yàng
这 件 上 衣 怎 么 样 ?

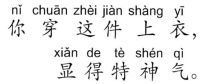

nǐ chuān zhèi jiàn shàng yī
你 穿 这 件 上 衣,
xiǎn de tè shén qì
显 得 特 神 气。

zhè dǐng mào zi zěn me yàng
这 顶 帽 子 怎 么 样 ?

nǐ dài zhèi dǐng mào zi
你 戴 这 顶 帽 子,
xiǎn de tǐng lǎo qì
显 得 挺 老 气。

zhè tiáo kù zǐ zěn me yàng
这 条 裤 子 怎 么 样 ?

nǐ chuān zhèi tiáo kù zi
你 穿 这 条 裤 子,
xiǎn de tài tǔ qì
显 得 太 土 气。

zhè fù yǎn jìng zěn me yàng
这 副 眼 镜 怎 么 样 ?

nǐ dài zhèi fù yǎn jìng
你 戴 这 副 眼 镜,
xiǎn de shū shēng qì
显 得 书 生 气。

zhè ge pí bāo zěn me yàng
这 个 皮 包 怎 么 样 ?

nǐ līn zhèi ge pí bāo
你 拎 这 个 皮 包,
xiǎn de bèi er shǎ qì
显 得 倍 儿 傻 气。

nǐ kàn wǒ zěn me yàng
你 看 我 怎 么 样 ?

nǐ de yì jǔ yí dòng
你 的 一 举 一 动,
dōu tài hái zi qì
都 太 孩 子 气。

Key words

1	怎么样？	zěnmeyàng	How about...?
2	显得	xiǎnde	it seems
3	特	tè	very
4	神气	shénqì	impressive
5	土气	tǔqì	similar to a country pumpkin
6	戴	dài	to wear (accessories)
7	挺	tǐng	very
8	老气	lǎoqì	old-fashioned
9	眼镜	yǎnjìng	eye glasses
10	书生气	shūshēngqì	scholarly looking
11	拎	līn	to carry
12	皮包	píbāo	briefcase
13	倍	bèi	so; extremely
14	傻气	shǎqì	foolish
15	一举一动	yìjǔyídòng	each and every move
16	孩子气	háiziqì	childish
17	看起来	kànqǐlái	to appear; to look as if
18	项链	xiàngliàn	necklace
19	领带	lǐngdài	tie

Let the words flow!

jīn wǎn wǒ qù tiào wǔ
今 晚 我 去 跳 舞,

wǒ chuān zhèi gè zěn me yàng
我 穿 这 个 怎 么 样?

nǐ zhèi jiàn chèn shān yòu xiǎo yòu shòu
你 这 件 衬 衫 又 小 又 瘦,

zhèi tiáo qún zi tài cháng
这 条 裙 子 太 长!

nǐ zhèi jiàn máo yī yòu féi yòu dà
你 这 件 毛 衣 又 肥 又 大,

wéi jīn de yán sè tài liàng
围 巾 的 颜 色 太 亮!

nà xiàn zài ne
那 现 在 呢?

wǒ jué de hái shì bú gòu piào liang
我 觉 得 还 是 不 够 漂 亮!

nǐ de méi máo yòu cū yòu duǎn
你 的 眉 毛 又 粗 又 短,

tóu fà yòu duō yòu juǎn
头 发 又 多 又 卷,

nǐ de bó zi yòu xì yòu cháng
你 的 脖 子 又 细 又 长,

tuǐ yě zhǎng de nán kàn
腿 也 长 得 难 看!

nà wǒ gāi zěn me bàn
那 我 该 怎 么 办?!

yào bú zán liǎ xià qí ba
要 不, 咱 俩 下 棋 吧。

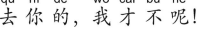

qù nǐ de wǒ cái bú ne
去 你 的, 我 才 不 呢!

Key words

1	跳舞	tiàowǔ	to dance
2	又…又	yòu…yòu…	both…and…
3	围巾	wéijīn	scarf
4	亮	liàng	bright (color)
5	觉得	juéde	to feel
6	够	gòu	enough
7	漂亮	piàoliang	beautiful; pretty
8	粗	cū	rough; thick
9	脖子	bózi	neck
10	细	xì	thin; delicate
11	难看	nánkàn	ugly
12	怎么办	zěnmebàn	What can be done?
13	要不	yàobú	How about…? otherwise
14	下棋	xiàqí	to play chess
15	去你的	qùnǐde	Get lost! Go away!
16	小气	xiǎoqì	stingy
17	大方	dàfāng	generous
18	热心	rèxīn	warm-hearted
19	倔	juè	stubborn

Language Focus

7.1 Vocabulary Review.

Read it aloud. Translate it into English.
Write it in Chinese characters, and say it aloud again as you write it.

	English	**Chinese**
1. 今晚还是明晚?	_____	_____
2. 显得书生气	_____	_____
3. 难看死了!	_____	_____
4. 裤子又肥又长!	_____	_____
5. 去你的!	_____	_____
6. 他的一举一动	_____	_____
7. 还是不够好。	_____	_____
8. 挺神气!	_____	_____
9. 跟朋友下棋	_____	_____
10. 漂亮的围巾	_____	_____
11. 细胳膊细腿	_____	_____
12. 颜色太亮了!	_____	_____
13. 戴眼镜的律师	_____	_____
14. 够了! 够了!	_____	_____

 Most of what you learn takes place in the classroom. So it is smart to know how to listen and how to take notes. Good note-taking is a skill that comes with practice. Writing things down reinforces what you hear and helps you remember.

7.2 Grammar Review: The use of 穿 & 戴.

穿 chuān: to wear, to put on clothes, shoes, socks, etc..

戴 dài: to wear, to put on a hat, glasses, gloves, tie, jewelry (accessories)…

穿 or 戴?

Describe the pictures using 穿 and 戴.

1. 穿球鞋

2. _____

3. _____

4. _____

5. _____

6. _____

7. _____

8. _____

9. _____

7.3 Grammar: The use of 又…又…

"又…又…" means "both…and…" in English.

Example: 1. 她又高又瘦。She is tall and slim.

2. 围巾又好看又便宜。The scarf is pretty and inexpensive.

3. 他又累又饿。He is tired and hungry.

| 1 警察　矮&胖 | 2 房子　小&旧 | 3 马　累&渴 |
| 4 写汉字　快&好看 | 5 Add your own | 6 Add your own |

Now use the above words to describe the pictures using 又…又….

1. _____

2. _____

3. _____

4. _____

5. _____

6. _____

7.4 Grammar: The use of 长得

长得：to look like

1. 他长得什么样？ What does he look like?

2. 他长得又高又帅。 He is tall and handsome.

长得像 xiàng：to take after; to resemble

1. 他长得像他爸不像他妈。

He looks like his father, not his mother.

2. 你长得像谁？

Who do you take after?

他长得什么样？

1. _____

2. _____

3. _____

回答问题：

1. 你长得像谁？ _____

_____

2. 谁长得最像你妈妈？ _____

_____

7.5 Opinion Survey.

同意还是不同意？

Compare your opinion with your classmate.

	看法	同意	不同意
1	汉语比法语更有用。		
2	科学比数学难学。		
3	人们更喜欢星期六。		
4	汉堡包没有热狗好吃。		
5	日本车比美国车又便宜又好。		
6	电子书比纸书好。		
7	上网比看电视有意思。		
8	人们每天应该睡八个小时。		
9	想要瘦，少吃糖，少吃肉。		

7.6 Give suggestions to these people.

1	2	3
谢万又胖了。	大海老饿。	艾米又没钱了。

1. _____

2. _____

3. _____

7.7 What's the questions?

什么问题?

Look at the answers. Write the questions.
Then compare them with your classmate.

1 马马虎虎。	2 厕所在书房旁边。
3 太难看啦!	4 我还没想好呢。
5 你应该少喝可乐。	6 去你家? 那我买吃的吧。
7 你戴眼镜好看。	8 不去! 你没看见我在忙吗!

1. _____

2. _____

3. _____

4. _____

5. _____

6. _____

7. _____

8. _____

7.8 Reading & Speaking

夏美眉问车雨红：我可以用你的电子书吗？雨红说：拿去用吧。**不一会儿**，美眉又问雨红：我能**借**你的笔刀吗？雨红说：可以，别忘了**还**我。

美眉和雨红是好朋友。美眉什么都好，可只有一点不好：她老是跟雨红借东西。美眉跟雨红借书，借笔，借笔刀，借手机，借电脑，借衣服什么的。虽然雨红心里不太高兴，可她什么都没说，还是美眉跟她借什么她都借给她。

一天，美眉和雨红吃完午饭回到教室。美眉说：我能借你的手机吗？雨红借给了美眉她的手机。不一会，美眉说：我有点儿冷，能借你的毛衣吗？雨红借给了美眉她的毛衣。快要放学了，美眉又问雨红：可以用一下儿你的**口红**吗？**这次**，雨红生气了。雨红大声对美眉说：你怎么老是跟我借东西?! 你该带你的书，你的笔，你的笔刀。你该用你自己的手机，穿你自己的衣服，用你自己的口红！对不起，我什么都可以借给你，可是，你不可以用我的口红！

美眉说：好啦，好啦，我知道啦！你的脸好红好红，要不要借我的**镜子**照照？

不一会儿 bùyíhuìr / shortly;　借 jiè / to borrow or lend;　还 huán / to return

口红 kǒuhóng / lipstick;　这次 zhècì / this time;　镜子 jìngzi / mirror

7.9 Fun with Chinese radicals

 A Chinese character often represents a part of history, an image, an idea, or an attitude about life.

For example, the character for island is 岛. It consists of two parts: 鸟 (bird) and 山 (mountain). Sea-birds often nest on mountainous rocks that emerge from the sea.

纟	Write down the characters with 纟 in it.
纟 is related to silk or thread, and is always placed on the left side.	
穴	Write down the characters with 穴 in it.
穴 is related to cave, and is always placed on the top.	

7.10 word detective Not so new

Here are some basic Chinese characters you have learned.
Let's see if you can decode their meanings.

	Pinyin	English	Make a sentence
1. 口香糖	_____	_____	_____
2. 围棋	_____	_____	_____
3. 借口	_____	_____	_____

Culture Focus

In many Asian cultures, the goal of communication is to achieve consensus of opinion and to promote group harmony. No means No. However, what does "Yes" mean in the Chinese culture? How can you tell when "Yes" really means "No"?

8　真的吗？　**Really?**

Everyone has feelings.　We experience different feelings during the day.　And we get to know ourselves through our feelings.

nǐ zěn me le
你 怎 么 了？

hǎo xiàng bù zěn me kāi xīn
好 像 不 怎 么 开 心。

nǐ hǎo xiàng yě bù kāi xīn
你 好 像 也 不 开 心。

wǒ zhēn de hěn shēng qì
我 真 的 很 生 气！

wǒ zuò cuò le sān dào tí
我 做 错 了 三 道 题。

wǒ zhēn de hěn nán guò
我 真 的 很 难 过！

tā kāi huài le wǒ de chē
他 开 坏 了 我 的 车。

wǒ zhēn de hěn hài pà
我 真 的 很 害 怕。

wǒ pà bèi jiào liàn mà
我 怕 被 教 练 骂。

wǒ zhēn de hěn fán nǎo
我 真 的 很 烦 恼！

wǒ yòu méi ná dào jià zhào
我 又 没 拿 到 驾 照。

wǒ zhēn de hěn gān gà
我 真 的 很 尴 尬。

wǒ yòu méi kǎo hǎo shēng huà
我 又 没 考 好 生 化。

wǒ zhēn de hěn chī jīng
我 真 的 很 吃 惊。

tā yào zǒu zhe qù běi jīng
他 要 走 着 去 北 京。

zhēn de　jiǎ de
真 的？假 的？

Key words

1	好像	hǎoxiàng	it seem
2	开心	kāixīn	happy; glad
3	生气	shēngqì	angry
4	做错	zuòcuò	did (it) incorrectly; did (it) wrong
5	题	tí	questions on a test
6	难过	nánguò	to feel sad; upset
7	坏	huài	broken
8	害怕	hàipà	to be afraid
9	被	bèi	by (indicates passive-voice)
10	教练	jiàoliàn	coach
11	烦恼	fánnǎo	to feel irritating
12	驾照	jiàzhào	driver's license
13	感到	gǎndào	to feel; to have the feeling of
14	尴尬	gāngà	to feel embarrassed; awkward
15	生化	shēnghuà	biochemistry
16	吃惊	chījīng	to be shocked
17	走	zǒu	to walk; to leave
18	着	zhe	a particle after a verb to indicate an action in progress
19	假	jiǎ	false

Let the words flow!

There are many good reasons in being a middle child. One of the advantages is the love you receive from both sides. Agree or disagree?

shuí rě nǐ la
谁 惹 你 啦?

bù gōng píng   bù gōng píng
不 公 平! 不 公 平!

zhēn shì bù gōng píng
真 是 不 公 平!

shàng yǒu dà   xià yǒu xiǎo
上 有 大, 下 有 小,

zhōng jiān de wèi zhì zuì bù hǎo
中 间 的 位 置 最 不 好。

shén me dōu shì èr shǒu huò
什 么 都 是 二 手 货,

nǐ shuō fán nǎo bù fán nǎo
你 说 烦 恼 不 烦 恼!

èr shǒu wán jù hé shū bāo
二 手 玩 具 和 书 包!

èr shǒu yī fú hé xié mào
二 手 衣 服 和 鞋 帽!

èr shǒu diàn shì hé jí tā
二 手 电 视 和 吉 他,

èr shǒu qì chē hé diàn nǎo
二 手 汽 车 和 电 脑!

suàn la   suàn la   bié shuō la
算 啦! 算 啦! 别 说 啦!

shuí ràng nǐ shì lǎo èr ne
谁 让 你 是 老 二 呢?

nǐ jiù rèn le ba
你 就 认 了 吧。

Key words

1	惹	rě	to bother; to cause (trouble)
2	公平	gōngpíng	fair
3	位置	wèizhì	position
4	二手	èrshǒu	second-hand
5	货	huò	stuff; things
6	玩具	wánjù	toy
7	汽车	qìchē	car
8	算啦!	suàn la	Let it go!
9	让	ràng	to let; to allow
10	老二	lǎoèr	the second child; the middle child
11	认	rèn	to admit; to recognize; to accept
12	家务活	jiāwùhuó	household chores
13	老大	lǎodà	the first child; leader of a group
14	老小	lǎoxiǎo	the youngest child
15	独生子	dúshēngzǐ	the only son
16	独生女	dúshēngnǚ	the only daughter
17	偏心	piānxīn	biased
18	唠叨	lāodào	to nag
19	地位	dìwèi	position; status

Language Focus

8.1 Vocabulary Review.

Read it aloud. Translate it into English.
Write it in Chinese characters, and say it aloud again as you write it.

	English	**Chinese**
1. 好像有问题	_____	_____
2. 为什么不开心?	_____	_____
3. 你在跟谁生气?	_____	_____
4. 特怕教练骂我。	_____	_____
5. 太让我心烦了!	_____	_____
6. 没拿到驾照	_____	_____
7. 真的? 假的?	_____	_____
8. 谁又惹你啦?	_____	_____
9. 一点儿不公平!	_____	_____
10. 二手车便宜。	_____	_____
11. 算啦! 算啦!	_____	_____
12. 高高兴兴	_____	_____
13. 让他说完。	_____	_____
14. 你就认了吧。	_____	_____

 Do you think that people choose to feel emotions or that the emotions happen to them? Why?

8.2 Vocabulary Review.

他们怎么样？

You may use a word more than once.

开心，生气，难过，害怕，烦恼，尴尬，吃惊，

高兴，着急，担心，后怕，感动，不好意思，惊喜，

1 老师说小美懒。
她 _____

2 夏冬忘了回电话。
他_____

3 丽丽的车坏了。
她_____

4 谢明明过生日。
他_____

5 厕所没手纸了。
他_____

6 猫想吃鱼。
鱼 _____

7 马跟妈要钱。
妈妈_____

8 大山不给狗比萨。
狗 _____

9 李超做不完作业。
他 _____

8.3 家树

你在哪儿？

Decorate your family tree. Add a person, add a leaf and add a fruit.

请你把家人画在树上。别忘了画你自己。

1. 你家人叫你什么？　＿＿＿＿＿＿＿＿＿＿＿＿＿＿

2. 你怎么知道家人的感觉？＿＿＿＿＿＿＿＿＿＿＿＿

3. 有事儿你喜欢跟谁说？　＿＿＿＿＿＿＿＿＿＿＿＿＿

4. 谁老惹你？　＿＿＿＿＿＿＿＿＿＿＿＿＿＿＿＿

5. 你觉得你爸妈公平吗？　＿＿＿＿＿＿＿＿＿＿＿＿＿

8.4 Grammar Review: The resultative complements

When you want to indicate the result of an action, a resultative complement is placed after a verb of action. Please remember only stative verbs and verbs can be used as resultative complements.

对 duì	correct 说对，做对，写对，买对	数学题他都做对了。
错 cuò	wrong 写错，做错，看错，听错	对不起，我做错作业了。
好 hǎo	properly, in a proper way 坐好，拿好，写好，想好	上课啦，请大家坐好。
坏 huài	broken, bad 用坏，穿坏，看坏，骑坏	我哥用坏了我的电脑。
清楚 qīngchǔ	clear 说清楚，看清楚，听清楚	看清楚了再写。
干净 gānjìng	clean 收拾干净，洗干净，	手洗干净了吗?
死 sǐ	_____ to die; death 忙死了，渴死了，急死了	气死我了!
会 huì	to master a skill 学会	我学会了开车。
见 jiàn	to have seen, heard 听见，看见	我听见有人说话。
到 dào	1) to have done something, 　找到，买到，想到， 2) to reach a place, a time, 　a level 　看到，学到，走到，	我找到了我的手机。 我们学到了第三课。
懂 dǒng	to understand 听懂，看懂，	老师说的我都听懂了。
完 wán	to finish 看完，吃完，做完，	我做完了汉语作业。
走 zǒu	to make something away 拿走，借走，带走，	大伟骑走了我的车。

8.5 What a terrible day!

We all have lousy days. So what can you do when the universe seems to conspire to make your life unpleasant? Try to say as much as you possibly can.

糟糕的一天！

今天，高老师的学生一进教室就说他们昨天过得有多不好。他们说什么了呢？

开心，生气，难过，害怕，烦恼，尴尬，吃惊，

高兴，着急，担心，后怕，感动，不好意思，惊喜，

1 夏红找不到手机。	2 狗吃了海浪的作业。
3 钱新的爸妈骂他笨蛋！	4 王小明的钱没了。
5 张早的女朋友要和他分手。	6 Add your own

Think about a time you were upset or frustrated. What was the problem? How did you feel about it? What did you do about it?

8.6 Work in pairs.

你又怎么啦?

我有<u>白头发</u>了。

有<u>白头发</u>了怕什么?

不怕什么,
我只是担心。

担心什么?

担心我老了。

1	2	3

戴眼镜	忘了喂狗	没做作业

8.7 Work in pairs.

你怎么了?

没怎么呀!

你<u>叫错了我的名字</u>!

叫错了你的名字?

你叫我谢大明了。

真的吗? 不会吧!

1	2	3

吃了别人的菜	拿错了手机	骑错了车。

8.8 家务活 – Chores around the house

Chores are commonly assigned by parents as tasks for children to complete around the house. The parents give their child or children chores as a way of learning disciplinary skills. Some parents utilize chores as a way for children to earn an allowance in order to create a connection between hard work and reward. Other parents believe that chores should be done as a family contribution and not for compensation.

你家谁做这些？

你常帮爸妈做什么？

1 喂鸭	2 打扫浴室	3 买菜
4 做饭	5 洗车	6 洗衣服
7 遛狗	8 Add your own	9 Add your own

8.9 回答问题.

Try to say as much as you possibly can.

1. 你家谁最爱生气？因为什么？ _____

2. 你的好朋友谁最开心？ _____

3. 你的老师谁最喜欢骂学生？ _____

4. 你哪个老师的心肠最好？ _____

5. 你最害怕什么？因为什么？ _____

6. 你爸妈最担心什么？ _____

7. 你的汉语老师为什么着急？ _____

8. 说一件让你感到最尴尬的事儿。 _____

9. 你做什么让你爸妈吃惊？ _____

10. 你妈常唠叨你什么？你听吗？ _____

8.10 **word detective** Not so new

Here are some basic Chinese characters you have learned.
Let's see if you can decode their meanings.

	Pinyin	English	Make a sentence
1. 坏人	_____	_____	_____
2. 难看	_____	_____	_____
3. 小人	_____	_____	_____
4. 生人	_____	_____	_____

8.11 Give advice to the people in the pictures.

It is an honor to be asked for advice, but it is also a big responsibility. Good advice can help people make sound decisions, while bad advice can have disastrous consequences.

1 包大海害怕考试。

2 高小红担心狗吃她的作业。

3 胖警察不想再胖了。

4 张早的女朋友又骂他来晚了。

5 大朋的书包又大又重。

6 李明老是做不好饭。

7 石牛上课睡觉惹老师生气。

8 夏美又找不到手机了。

高老师很生气。她生学生的气。她不知道今天学生都怎么了。他们**平时**都很听话，都是好学生，可今天他们都不**听话**。大明上课**不但**不注意听，**而且**还睡觉。李超不但没做作业，而且还上课说话。艾米不但忘了带她的汉语书，而且还上课喝可乐。丽丽不但不回答问题，而且还吃三明治。李朋上课来晚了，他说他妈忘了叫他起床了。还有，王星上汉语课写历史报告。李开来上课玩手机里的**游戏**，因为他觉得他会说汉语。高小红不知道为什么没来，可能还在家睡觉吧。今天很多学生都没有做完作业。高老师心里很烦。

高老师下班回到家什么都不想干。她觉得很累。她的学生今天都不听话，这让她很难过！高老师累得不想做饭，不想带狗出去走，不想给朋友打电话，不想上网，也不想看书。她累得什么都不想做。高老师坐在**沙发**上说：今儿学生都怎么了？教书真难！不过，高老师喜欢**教书**，喜欢她的学生。高老师**希望**学生每天都听她的话，都能做完作业。高老师觉得很累。她今晚什么都不做，只想听听歌看看电视什么的。

平时 píngshí / usually; 不但…，而且 érqiě… / not only…, but also…;

听话 tīnghuà / to obey; 游戏 yóuxì / games; 沙发 shāfā / sofa;

教书 jiāoshū / to teach; 希望 xīwàng / to wish

8.13 Fun with Chinese radicals

 A Chinese character often represents a part of history, an image, an idea, or an attitude about life.

For example, the character for poor is 贫. It consists of two parts:

分 (to divide) and 贝 (shells once used as money in ancient China).

心	Write down the characters with 心 in it.
心 is related to feelings or heart. It is always placed at the bottom.	
忄	Write down the characters with 忄 in it.
忄 is related to heart or feelings, and is always placed on the left side.	

Culture Focus

The dictionary defines culture as the arts, beliefs, customs, institutions and all other products of human work and thought created by a people or group. Chinese culture is rich in all of these, and it dates back thousands of years.

There is nothing more important than "face" in Chinese culture. The Chinese concept of face is associated with honor, dignity, and a deep sense of pride. In Chinese culture, losing face, saving face and giving face is very important and should never be forgotten.

1. How does "Face" work in everyday life?

_____

_____

2. Have you ever seen "Face" play around you? If yes, how?

_____

我病了。 **I am sick.**

This rhyme is a fun exercise for you and your classmates to do between classes or even during class when you feel a little sleepy. So, get up and stretch!

jǔ qǐ yòu shǒu   jǔ qǐ zuǒ shǒu
举 起 右 手。举 起 左 手。

pāi pāi shuāng shǒu   fàng xià shǒu
拍 拍 双 手。放 下 手。

shēn chū yòu shǒu   pāi pāi zuǒ jiān
伸 出 右 手，拍 拍 左 肩。

shēn chū zuǒ shǒu   pāi pāi yòu jiān
伸 出 左 手，拍 拍 右 肩。

duò duò yòu jiǎo   duò duò zuǒ jiǎo
跺 跺 右 脚。跺 跺 左 脚。

yī èr sān sì   bèng bèng tiào tiào
一 二 三 四，蹦 蹦 跳 跳。

wān xià shēn zi   mō mō jiǎo zhǐ
弯 下 身 子，摸 摸 脚 趾。

zhí qǐ shēn lái   yáo yáo nǎo dài
直 起 身 来，摇 摇 脑 袋。

wǎng qián zǒu zǒu   wǎng hòu tuì tuì
往 前 走 走，往 后 退 退。

Lǎo shī xué shēng   qǐng huí zuò wèi
老 师 学 生，请 回 座 位。

Key words

1	双	shuāng	pair; two; double
2	放下	fàngxià	to put down
3	伸出	shēnchū	to stretch; to extend
4	肩	jiān	shoulder
5	跺	duò	to stamp one's feet
6	蹦	bèng	to hop
7	跳	tiào	to jump
8	弯下	wānxià	to bend down
9	身子	shēnzi	body
10	摸	mō	to touch
11	脚趾	jiǎozhi	toe
12	直	zhí	to straighten; straight
13	摇	yáo	to shake; to rock; to row
14	脑袋	nǎodai	head
15	往	wǎng	to go towards a (direction)
16	退	tuì	to go back; to retreat
17	座位	zuòwèi	seat
18	屁股	pìgu	butt
19	背	bèi	back

Let the words flow!

头疼 tóuténg headache	嗓子疼 sǎngzi téng sore throat	咳嗽 késou cough	拉肚子 lā dùzi diarrhea	发烧 fāshāo fever

nǐ nǎ er bù shū fú
你 哪 儿 不 舒 服？

wǒ dù zi yǒu diǎn er téng
我 肚 子 有 点 儿 疼。

kàn le yī sheng méi yǒu
看 了 医 生 没 有？

kàn le yě méi yòng
看 了 也 没 用。

nà shì wèi shén me
那 是 为 什 么？

wǒ chī le bīng qí lín
我 吃 了 冰 淇 淋！

chī le bīng qí lín
吃 了 冰 淇 淋？

tài duō de bīng qí lín
太 多 的 冰 淇 淋！

nǐ yòu zěn me le
你 又 怎 么 了？

wǒ de yá yǒu diǎn er téng
我 的 牙 有 点 儿 疼。

kàn le yī sheng méi yǒu
看 了 医 生 没 有？

Kàn le yě méi yòng
看 了 也 没 用。

nà shì wèi shén me
那 是 为 什 么？

wǒ chī le tài duō de bīng qí lín
我 吃 了 太 多 的 冰 淇 淋！

Key words

1	病	bìng	sick
2	疼	téng	hurt; sore
3	嗓子	sǎngzi	throat
4	咳嗽	késou	cough
5	拉肚子	lādùzi	diarrhea
6	发烧	fāshāo	to have a temperature
7	舒服	shūfu	comfortable
8	没用	méiyòng	not necessary; useless
9	冰淇淋	bīngqílín	ice cream
10	痛	tòng	hurt; sore
11	量	liáng	to measure
12	体温	tǐwēn	body temperature
13	体重	tǐzhòng	body weight
14	医院	yīyuàn	hospital
15	过敏	guòmǐn	to be allergic; allergy
16	失眠	shīmián	insomnia
17	肥胖病	féipàngbìng	obesity
18	急诊室	jízhěnshì	emergency room
19	看急诊	kànjízhěn	to go to the emergency room

Language Focus

9.1 Vocabulary Review.

Read it aloud. Translate it into English.
Write it in Chinese characters, and say it aloud again as you write it.

	English	**Chinese**
1. 我病了。	_____	_____
2. 哪儿都不舒服。	_____	_____
3. 头疼脑	_____	_____
4. 看了医生没有？	_____	_____
5. 最怕生病住院	_____	_____
6. 快回座位！	_____	_____
7. 疼死我了！	_____	_____
8. 头疼了一天	_____	_____
9. 发高烧	_____	_____
10. 有点儿低热	_____	_____
11. 肥胖病	_____	_____
12. 小毛病没事。	_____	_____
13. 去医院看病	_____	_____
14. 病从口入。	_____	_____

 There are three ways your doctor can help you stay healthy – prevention, screening and treatment. Unfortunately, many people see their doctors only to get treated when they are sick.

9.2 Vocabulary Review.

Label the body parts

手，脸，头or脑袋，头发，眼睛，眉毛，鼻子，嘴，

耳朵，肩，胳膊，肚子，腿，脚，脚趾，身子，

9.3 Too sick to go to school?

他们没来上学！

高老师今天没给学生考试，因为她有好几个学生不在。他们为什么没来上学呢？他们没来是因为有病还是因为怕考试呢？你觉得他们谁应该上学？

1 王大明头疼。	2 李超嗓子疼。	3 黄小春咳嗽。
4 老牛胳膊疼。	5 石可可拉肚子。	6 丽哪儿都不舒服。
7 夏美红牙疼。	8 包新新发烧。	9 白小秋肚子疼。

Call in sick or go to school?

How do you know when you are too sick to come to school to take a test? Discuss it with your classmates.

9.4 Give advice.

People have different remedies for medical problems that are not too serious. For example, people do different things when they burn a finger or have a bloody nose.

Practice having conversations with your classmates.
What special remedies do you use when you are sick.

1 头疼	2 嗓子疼	3 牙疼
4 发烧	5 拉肚子	6 老是担心

1. _____

2. _____

3. _____

4. _____

5. _____

6. _____

9.5 Grammar: The directional complement: 来, 去

To indicate if an action is moving towards the speaker or away from the speaker, a "directional complement" is attached to the action verb.

If the motion is towards the speaker, the complement 来 (to come) is used.

If the motion is away from the speaker, the complement 去 (to go) is used.

For example: 妈妈拿去了我的手机。
Mom took my cell phone away. (The speaker does not have the phone)

老师买来了一些书。
The teacher bought some books. (The speaker and the teacher are together)

来 and 去 often appear with the following motion verbs:

上	下	进	出	回	过	起
shàng	xià	jìn	chū	huí	guò	qǐ
upward	downward	inward	outward	return	cross	raise

	上	下	进	出	回	过	起
来	上来 to come up	下来 to come down	进来 to come in	出来 to come out	回来 to come back	过来 to come here	起来 to raise up
去	上去 to go up	下去 to go down	进去 to go in	出去 to go out	回去 to go back	过去 to go over	

For example:　请坐下。　　　　　　Please sit down.

他从中国回来了。　　He returned from China.

他拿出了手机。　　　He took out his cell phone.

老师要我们进去。　　Teacher told us to go in.

起床!　　　　　　　Get up! Or get out your bed!

9.6 Grammar Review: The directional complements

上	下	进	出	回	过	起
shàng	xià	jìn	chū	huí	guò	qǐ
upward	downward	inward	outward	return	cross	raise

	上	下	进	出	回	过	起
来	上来 to come up	下来 to come down	进来 to come in	出来 to come out	回来 to come back	过来 to come here	起来 to raise up
去	上去 to go up	下去 to go down	进去 to go in	出去 to go out	回去 to go back	过去 to go over	

Translate the following sentences.

1. 老师让大家都进去。 _____

2. 我女朋友买衣服去了。 _____

3. 吉他你从哪儿借来的？ _____

4. 金毛狗喜欢跑来跑去。 _____

5. 老师不要我们站起来。 _____

6. 丽丽的车被小明骑去了。 _____

7. 妈妈给我请来了家教。 _____

8. 大家从这儿下去吧。 _____

9. 她从卧室走出来了。 _____

10. 他走过来拿书包。 _____

11. 丽丽被老师叫出去了。 _____

9.7 Work in pairs.

你昨天怎么没来?

好点儿了没有?

我病了,
头疼了一天。

好多了,
只是还不想吃饭。

只要头不疼了就好。

1	2	3

嗓子疼	咳嗽	牙疼

9.8 Word detective — Not so new

Here are some basic Chinese characters you have learned.
Let's see if you can decode their meanings.

	Pinyin	English	Make a sentence
1. 牙医	_____	_____	_____
2. 学医	_____	_____	_____
3. 中医	_____	_____	_____
4. 西医	_____	_____	_____

9.9 Good habits or bad habits?

	Habits	好	不好
1	我很少吃早饭，因为我早上起不来。		
2	我每个星期洗两次澡。		
3	我每次吃完饭都刷牙。		
4	我常吃肉，很少吃菜。		
5	我每次吃饭前都洗手。		
6	我非常喜欢吃甜点。		
7	我每天最少喝五杯咖啡。		
8	我每天要看四个多小时的电视。		
9	我周末常睡到下午才起床。		
10	想运动就运动，不想运动就不运动。		

Forming good habits is an important part of living a good life.

9.10 Body moment

	Movement
眼睛	看，
嘴	说话，
手	写字，
脚	走，

9.11 Tic-Tac-Toe

What advice do you give for the problem in the picture? Draw an X or O over the picture when you make a sentence. Get three X's or O's in a row in any directions: horizontal, vertical, or diagonal. Whenever three matching symbols in a row are turned over by either player, the game ends.

1 王大明又没钱啦!	2 小明的书包太重!	3 美丽汉语说得不好。
4 王新雨快要忙死了!	5 她的学生不听话。	6 张海山老是饿。
7 李超早上起不来。	8 夏雪不喜欢牛牛。	9 棕马又累又渴。

Despite its simplicity, Tic-tac-toe requires analysis. The most interesting of which are the number of possible games and the number of possible positions.

丽丽十五岁，她有一个弟弟和一个妹妹。丽丽的弟弟叫小明，今年九岁，上三年级。丽丽的妹妹叫小美，今年五岁，还没上学。今天下大雪，丽丽和弟弟妹妹都不上学。丽丽的爸爸妈妈上午要去医院看丽丽的奶奶，所以，他们要丽丽帮助**照看**弟弟妹妹。

丽丽是个好姐姐，她什么都会做。她给弟弟妹妹念小人书。弟弟妹妹喜欢听什么她就给他们念什么。丽丽给弟弟妹妹做午饭。弟弟妹妹想吃什么她就给他们做什么。丽丽教弟弟妹妹唱歌。弟弟妹妹想要唱什么她就教他们什么。丽丽还跟弟弟妹妹玩游戏。弟弟妹妹想玩什么她就跟他们玩什么。丽丽真是个好姐姐。

妹妹说她想吃冰淇淋，然后就去厨房拿。**冰箱**高，妹妹拿来椅子站了上去。可是，**她摔**了下来。听见厨房有声音，丽丽和弟弟都跑进了厨房。他们看见妹妹**躺**在厨房的**地板**上。弟弟吓坏啦。丽丽知道她该怎么做。丽丽打了 **911**。几分钟以后，**救护车**就到了。大家都说丽丽做得对。

照看 zhàokàn / look after；冰箱 bīngxiāng / refrigerator；摔 shuāi / to fall；躺 tǎng / to lie down；地板 dìbǎn / floor；救护车 jiùhùchē / ambulance

9.13 Fun with Chinese radicals

A Chinese character often represents a part of history, an image, an idea, or an attitude about life.

For example, the character for to forget is 忘. It consists of two parts:

亡 (die or death) and 心 (heart).

疒	Write down the characters with 疒 in it.
疒 is related mostly to illness, and its position is fixed.	
月	Write down the characters with 月 in it.
月 on the left is related to flesh. 月 on the right is related to the moon.	

Culture Focus

The Five Elements Theory

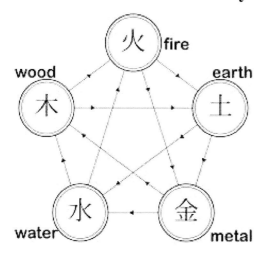

The Five Elements Theory is based on the idea that everything in nature, including the human body included, can be simplified into the five elements of wood, fire, earth, metal and water.

Organ Clock

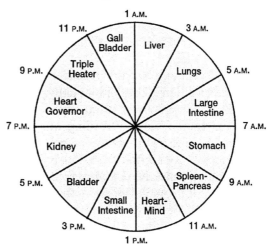

The layout of the clock is determined by the natural order of the energy flow through the body's system according to Chinese medicine.

China covers a large territory and has 56 nationalities. There is a wide variety of Chinese food, each with different but fantastic mouthwatering flavors.

nǐ zěn me le
你怎么了？

wǒ è le
我饿了。

nǐ xiǎng chī diǎn er shén me
你 想 吃 点 儿 什 么？

wǒ shén me dōu xiǎng chī   dàn chǎo fàn   niú ròu miàn   bāo zǐ
我 什 么 都 想 吃：蛋 炒 饭，牛 肉 面， 包 子，

jiǎo zǐ   suān là tāng   gōng bào jī dīng hé mǐ fàn
饺 子， 酸 辣 汤， 宫 爆 鸡 丁 和 米 饭。

nǐ zěn me le
你怎么了？

wǒ yǒu diǎn er kě
我 有 点 儿 渴。

nǐ xiǎng hē diǎn er shén me
你 想 喝 点 儿 什 么？

wǒ shén me dōu xiǎng hē   niú nǎi   kā fēi hé xuě bì
我 什 么 都 想 喝：牛 奶， 咖 啡 和 雪 碧。

kě lè   qì shuǐ hé qī xǐ   hái yǒu guǒ zhī   bīng chá hé
可 乐， 汽 水 和 七 喜。 还 有 果 汁， 冰 茶 和

qiǎo kè lì
巧 克 力。

qiǎo kè lì
巧 克 力？

qiǎo kè lì niú nǎi
巧 克 力 牛 奶。

Key words

1	饿	è	hungry
2	炒饭	chǎofàn	fried rice
3	包子	bāozi	steamed meat or vegetable ban
4	饺子	jiǎozi	dumpling
5	辣	là	spicy; hot
6	汤	tāng	soup
7	宫爆	gōngbào	kongpao
8	鸡丁	jīdīng	diced chicken meat
9	米饭	mǐfàn	cooked rice
10	渴	kě	thirsty
11	咖啡	kāfēi	coffee
12	汽水	qìshuǐ	soda water
13	请客	qǐngkè	to (invite) entertain guest
14	买单	mǎidān	to pay the bill in a restaurant
15	春卷	chūnjuǎn	spring roll
16	豆腐	dòufu	tofu
17	付钱	fùqián	to pay (bill)
18	吃素	chīsù	to be a vegetarian
19	随便	suíbiàn	as one please; as you wish

Let the words flow!

We all love fruit. In the Chinese culture, people often eat fresh fruit as dessert.

nǐ mài shuǐ guǒ ma
你 卖 水 果 吗?

nǐ dōu mài xiē shá
你 都 卖 些 啥?

dāng rán la　dāng rán la
当 然 啦! 当 然 啦!

wǒ zhè er yǒu
我 这 儿 有:

píng guǒ yā lí hé jú zi
苹 果 鸭 梨 和 橘 子,

bō luó xiāng jiāo hé lǐ zi
菠 萝 香 蕉 和 李 子,

pú táo máng guǒ hé táo zi
葡 萄 芒 果 和 桃 子,

yīng táo cǎo méi hé yē zi
樱 桃 草 莓 和 椰 子。

yǒu xī guā ma
有 西 瓜 吗?

dāng rán la　dāng rán la
当 然 啦! 当 然 啦!

hái yǒu
还 有:

mù guā níng méng hé xìng zǐ
木 瓜 柠 檬 和 杏 子。

nǐ de shuǐ guǒ tián bù tián
你 的 水 果 甜 不 甜?

dōu hěn tián　dōu hěn tián
都 很 甜! 都 很 甜!

suān le bú yào nǐ yì fēn qián
酸 了 不 要 你 一 分 钱!

bù xìn　nǐ cháng chang
不 信, 你 尝 尝!

Key words

1	水果	shuǐguǒ	fruit
2	当然	dāngrán	Of course. certainly; with no doubt
3	鸭梨	yālí	pear
4	橘子	júzi	orange
5	菠萝	bōluó	pineapple
6	香蕉	xiāngjiāo	banana
7	桃子	táozi	peach
8	葡萄	pútao	grape
9	芒果	mángguǒ	mango
10	李子	lǐzi	plum
11	樱桃	yīngtáo	cherry
12	草莓	cǎoméi	strawberry
13	椰子	yēzi	coconut
14	木瓜	mùguā	papaya
15	杏子	xìngzi	apricot
16	信	xìn	to trust; to believe; letter
17	尝	cháng	to taste
18	生	shēng	raw
19	熟	shú	ripe

Language Focus

10.1 Vocabulary Review.

Read it aloud. Translate it into English.
Write it in Chinese characters, and say it aloud again as you write it.

	English	**Chinese**
1. 饿死我了！	_____	_____
2. 今天谁请客?	_____	_____
3. 我会做蛋炒饭。	_____	_____
4. 渴了什么都喝。	_____	_____
5. 我什么都想吃。	_____	_____
6. 春卷还是煎饺?	_____	_____
7. 来两碗牛肉面。	_____	_____
8. 喝咖啡不加糖	_____	_____
9. 我吃素，你呢?	_____	_____
10. 你该多吃菜。	_____	_____
11. 五颜六色的水果	_____	_____
12. 她做菜好吃。	_____	_____
13. 信不信?	_____	_____
14. 当然啦！	_____	_____

 Speak with your stomach!
In most cultures, meals are a social event. Even the shyest solo traveler is certain to interact with locals when ordering food and drinks.

10.2 Name that fruit.

You may use position words: 上面，下面，左边，右边...

For example: 香蕉下面是葡萄，上面是草莓。

什么水果？

1	2	3
4	5	6
7	8	9
10 Add your own	11 Add your own	12 Add your own

哪些水果跟苹果一起吃好吃？

人们用水果做什么？

10.3 Vocabulary review: Food

你有十五块钱，你会买什么？

1 茶蛋/¥1.50 个	2 春卷/¥4.50	3 包子/¥1.50 个	4 饺子/¥3.40
5 蛋花汤/¥4.90	6 柠檬鸡/¥9.99	7 烤鱼/¥12.99	8 炒面/¥6.70
9 汉堡包/¥21	10 热狗/¥7.50	11 比萨/¥14.50	12 三明治/¥9.50
13 蛋糕/¥21.50	14 羊肉串儿/¥5.50	15 烤鸭/¥120	16 Add your own

What can you buy for ¥25 ?

1. 你常去哪家中国饭店吃饭？ _____

2. 你最喜欢吃什么中国饭？ _____

3. 你家谁饭做得好吃？ _____

10.4 Vocabulary review: Drinks

你有十块钱，你会买什么？

1 咖啡/¥10	2 茶/¥3.50	3 水/不要钱	4 鲜果汁/¥10
5 橙汁/¥4.50	6 香蕉汁/¥5.60	7 苹果汁/¥3.50	8 西瓜汁/¥6.50
9 可乐/¥5.00	10 汽水/¥7.50	11 芬达/¥6.70	12 七喜/¥5.50
13 牛奶/¥3.50	14 红牛/¥10	Add your own	Add your own

What can you buy for ¥20 ?

1. 你早饭常喝什么？ _____

2. 你午饭常喝什么？ _____

3. 你晚饭常喝什么？ _____

10.5 What kind of meat do you like?

肉 ròu - meat

If you add 肉 after an animal, then it becomes the meat of that animal.

For example:　　　鸡肉，　　　牛肉，　　　猪肉
　　　　　　　　chicken meat　　　beef　　　　pork

1. I know how to cook a roasted turkey, and can do it very well.

_____

2. I don't like to eat meat. I am a vegetarian.

_____

3. You should eat more vegetables and less meat.

_____

4. Beijing duck is very delicious. You should try it.

_____

10.6 Food Smarts.

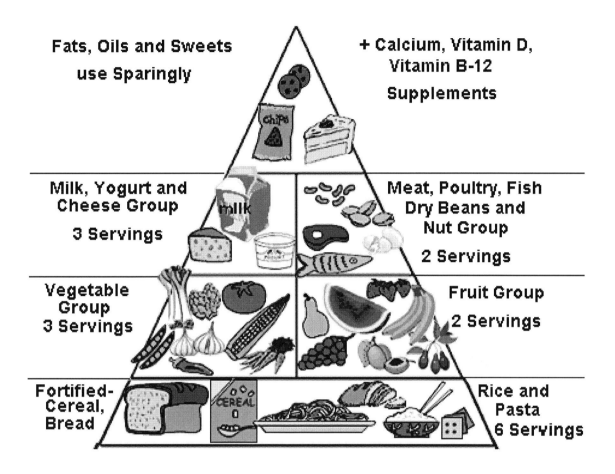

Do you have any healthy eating habits? Do you have any unhealthy habits you wish you could change? Think about what you or your family like. Can you or your family use some healthy suggestions?

	早饭	中饭	晚饭	小吃
Grains				
菜				
水果				
喝的				
肉				

10.7 Grammar: The complex directional complement

The complex directional complement is a very useful grammar in the Chinese language.

Review:

	上	下	进	出	回	过	起
来	上来 to come up	下来 to come down	进来 to come in	出来 to come out	回来 to come back	过来 to come here	起来 to raise up
去	上去 to go up	下去 to go down	进去 to go in	出去 to go out	回去 to go back	过去 to go over	

Verb + 上来，下来，进来，出来，回来，过来，起来
上去，下去，进去，出去，回去，过去，

For example: 她站起来说：你好!
She stood up and said: Hello!

请把书拿出来。
Take out your book, please.

老师要我们游过去。
The teacher told us to swim over (away from the teacher).

Translate the sentences.

1. Mom brought back hotdogs and Coke. _____

2. He took away my dictionary. _____

3. She cannot recall his name. _____

4. My dog ran out to get the magazine. _____

5. He took money out of his wallet. _____

6. Speak up when you have something to say! _____

10.8 The complex directional complement

Fill in the blanks with the directional complements

上来，下来，进来，出来，回来，回去，过来，起来，
上去，下去，进去，出去，过去，

1. 他从书包里拿_____ _____了电脑。

2. 这些苹果，你带_____ _____吃吧。

3. 请大家坐_____ _____说。

4. 弟弟从外面跑_____ _____找可乐喝。

5. 还剩一分钟，我踢_____ _____了一个球。

6. 请帮我把车上的东西拿_____ _____，好吗？

10.9 猜猜是什么吃的？

	问题	回答
1	北京有一道菜非常又名。	
2	中国老人过生日，你该送什么水果？	
3	在饭店吃饭，小姐会给客人上什么水果？	
4	过年的时候，桌上有一道菜不要吃完。	
5	中秋节，人们会吃一种什么点心？	
6	在中国，什么水果不要分着 (share) 吃？	
7	过年的时候，中国人喜欢在家里放什么果树？	

10.10 Work in pairs.

1. 在饭店吃饭

 请问，您想吃什么？

想喝点儿什么？

有花茶和绿茶。

猪肉饺子。

有茶吗？

我要绿茶。

1	2	3

炒面	三明治	羊肉串儿

2. 在饭馆吃饭

 请问，您想点什么？

对不起，酸辣汤没了。
蛋花汤可以吗？

您想喝点儿什么？

酸辣汤和**炒面**。

不要汤了，
只要**炒面**。

给我来杯**热水**吧。

1	2	3

柠檬鸡 / 花茶	烤鱼 / 七喜	包子 / 咖啡

10.11 Grammar review: The alternative question

An alternative question is formed of two statements joined by 还是 suggesting two different choices.

Example:　　　　你想喝可乐还是七喜？
Do you want to drink Coke or 7-Up?

你想吃比萨还是意大利面？
Do you want to eat pizza or Italian noodles?

1. Do you want to go to Beijing or Shanghai?　　　_____

2. Do you want to watch TV or play poker?　　　_____

3. Is he coming today or tomorrow?　　　_____

4. Does your teacher have a dog or a bird?　　　_____

10.12 Fun with Chinese radicals

A Chinese character often represents a part of history, an image, an idea, or an attitude about life.

For example, the character for thunder is 雷. It consists of two parts:

雨 (rain) and 田 (field). It means lighting flashes and thunder echoes in the field.

艹	Write down the characters with 艹 in it.
艹 is related mostly to plant or grass, and is always placed on the top.	
木	Write down the characters with 木 in it.
木 is related to wood or tree, and is usually placed on the left.	

丽丽渴了，她去厨房找东西喝。丽丽**打开**冰箱，见**冰箱**里有很多五颜六色的水果：红苹果，绿苹果，红葡萄，绿葡萄，黄香蕉，绿香蕉，黄鸭梨，绿鸭梨，红草莓，蓝草莓，还有黄菠萝和紫樱桃什么的。**虽然**这些五颜六色的水果好看，可是，丽丽不想吃水果。丽丽看见冰箱里有牛奶，可乐，冰茶和西瓜汁什么的，可是，这也不是她想要喝的。

丽丽看见冰箱里有**啤酒**。啤酒是爸爸喜欢喝的。丽丽的爸爸非常喜欢喝啤酒。他每天吃晚饭都要喝啤酒。丽丽没喝过啤酒，所以她不知道啤酒好不好喝。丽丽想如果爸爸每天都喝啤酒，那啤酒一定好喝啦。想到这儿，丽丽从冰箱里拿出一罐啤酒。她打开啤酒罐**闻**了闻，没什么**味儿**。她尝了一小口。呸！怎么这么**苦**啊！啤酒一点儿也不甜！啤酒一点儿也不酸！啤酒非常苦！好像还有点儿辣。啤酒这么不好喝，可是，爸爸为什么天天都喝啤酒呢？丽丽晚上要问爸爸为什么喜欢喝啤酒。最后，丽丽吃了个苹果，喝了杯巧克力牛奶。

打开 dǎkái / to open； 冰箱 bīngxiāng / refrigerator； 啤酒 píjiǔ / beer；

闻 wén / to smell； 味儿 wèi / smell or taste； 苦 kǔ / bitter； 辣 là / spicy；

10.14 word detective Not so new

Here are some basic Chinese characters you have learned.
Let's see if you can decode their meanings.

	Pinyin	English	Make a sentence
1. 奶茶	_____	_____	_____
2. 网吧	_____	_____	_____
3. 点心	_____	_____	_____

10.15 Each picture tells a story - - what's your story?

Use your imagination. Write as many sentences as you can.

_____

_____

_____

_____

Culture Focus

Table manners are the rules of etiquette used while eating. Different cultures observe different rules for table manners. What are the proper table manners in China?

People love to talk about weather. It is a way to start a conversation. Learn some common weather vocabulary and you will find it easy to start a conversation with anyone.

míng tiān tiān qì hǎo　míng tiān tiān qì qíng
明天天气好，明天天气晴，

wǒ men yì qǐ qù lù yíng　nǐ kàn xíng bù xíng
我们一起去露营，你看行不行？

míng tiān tiān qì rè　míng tiān tiān qì qíng
明天天气热，明天天气晴，

wǒ men yì qǐ qù chōng làng　nǐ kàn xíng bù xíng
我们一起去冲浪，你看行不行？

míng tiān méi yǒu yǔ　míng tiān tiān qì qíng
明天没有雨，明天天气晴，

wǒ men yì qǐ qù pān yán　nǐ kàn xíng bù xíng
我们一起去攀岩，你看行不行？

míng tiān bú xià xuě　míng tiān tiān qì qíng
明天不下雪，明天天气晴，

wǒ men yì qǐ qù huá xuě　nǐ kàn xíng bù xíng
我们一起去滑雪，你看行不行？

zhōu mò tiān qì lěng　tiān qì yě bù qíng
周末天气冷，天气也不晴，

wǒ men zài jiā kàn diàn shì　nǐ kàn xíng bù xíng
我们在家看电视，你看行不行？

xíng　xíng　xíng　xíng　xíng　xíng
行，行，行！行，行，行！

nǐ xiǎng zuò shén me dōu xíng
你想做什么都行！

Key words

1	天气	tiānqì	weather
2	晴	qíng	clear (weather)
3	露营	lùyíng	to camp out; camping
4	行	xíng	Ok.
5	雨	yǔ	rain
6	攀岩	pānyán	rock climbing
7	雪	xuě	snow
8	下雪	xiàxuě	to snow
9	预报	yùbào	forecast
10	气温	qìwēn	temperature
11	阳光	yángguāng	sunshine
12	阴天	yīntiān	cloudy
13	凉爽	liángshuǎng	cool
14	风	fēng	wind
15	雾	wù	fog
16	多云	duōyún	cloudy
17	阵雨	zhènyǔ	shower
18	毛毛雨	máomaoyǔ	drizzle
19	冰雹	bīngbáo	hail

Let the words flow!

nǐ zhōu mò cháng zuò shén me
你周末常做什么?

tiān qì rè de shí hòu　wǒ qí chē qù hǎi biān
天气热的时候，我骑车去海边。

tiān qì lěng de shí hòu　wǒ kāi chē qù tài shān
天气冷的时候，我开车去泰山。

tiān qì yīn de shí hòu　wǒ qí mǎ qù shì nèi
天气阴的时候，我骑马去市内。

xià dà yǔ de shí hòu　wǒ zuò chē yóu shān chuān
下大雨的时候，我坐车游山川。

nǐ zhōu mò zěn me guò ne
你周末怎么过呢?

tiān qì qíng de shí hòu　wǒ qù shān shàng zhòng shù
天气晴的时候，我去山上种树。

tiān qì liáng de shí hòu　wǒ qù xiāng xià sàn bù
天气凉的时候，我去乡下散步。

guā dà fēng de shí hòu　wǒ qù hǎi lǐ chōng làng
刮大风的时候，我去海里冲浪。

xià dà xuě de shí hòu　wǒ qù wài miàn sǎo lù
下大雪的时候，我去外面扫路。

míng tiān tiān qì hǎo　tiān yě tè bié qíng
明天天气好，天也特别晴，

wǒ men yì qǐ qù shāo kǎo
我们一起去烧烤，

nǐ kàn xíng bù xíng
你看行不行?

xíng　xíng　xíng　nǐ xiǎng gàn shén me dōu xíng
行，行，行! 你想干什么都行!

Key words

1	时候	shíhòu	moment
2	...的时候	deshíhòu	when
3	海边	hǎibiān	seaside
4	泰山	tàishān	Tai mountain
5	骑马	qímǎ	to ride a horse
6	市内	shìnèi	downtown; inner city
7	下雨	xiàyǔ	to rain
8	坐车	zuòchē	to take a bus, subway, train, etc.
9	游	yóu	to tour; to sightsee; to swim
10	山上	shānshàng	on top of the mountain
11	种树	zhòngshù	to plant trees
12	乡下	xiāngxià	countryside
13	散步	sànbù	to take a walk
14	刮风	guāfēng	windy
15	扫路	sǎolù	to sweep the road
16	特别	tèbié	especially; special; unusual
17	烧烤	shāokǎo	barbecue
18	郊游	jiāoyóu	outing; field-trip
19	夏令营	xiàlìngyíng	summer camp

Language Focus

11.1 Vocabulary Review.

Read it aloud. Translate it into English.
Write it in Chinese characters, and say it aloud as you write.

	English	**Chinese**
1. 天气不冷不热。	_____	_____
2. 晴天啦!	_____	_____
3. 行不行?	_____	_____
4. 周末做什么?	_____	_____
5. 什么时候走?	_____	_____
6. 下雪哪儿都别去。	_____	_____
7. 骑车去市内吧。	_____	_____
8. 去外面帮忙扫雪	_____	_____
9. 攀岩怕不怕?	_____	_____
10. 山上人多	_____	_____
11. 天气怎么样?	_____	_____
12. 特爽!	_____	_____
13. 冷了多穿点儿。	_____	_____
14. 常去公园散步	_____	_____

 The world is changing all the time, so words change too, to keep up with it. New words are being invented all the time. Some news words become part of a language, because they are useful, and others that are not so useful may be forgotten quickly.

11.2 Match the words and the pictures.

晴天，下雨， 冷，刮风，阴天，下雪，热，多云，

1 _____	2 _____	3 _____
4 Cloudy _____	5 _____	6 _____
7 _____	8 _____	9 Add your own

1. 昨天天气怎么样? _____

2. 今天的天气呢? _____

3. 你喜欢冷天还是热天? 为什么? _____

4. 如果周末下雨，你会做什么? _____

5. 夏天人们喜欢去哪儿? _____

6. 哪个季节的水果又多又好吃? _____

11.3 Activity Review 1

天气好的时候，人们去外面做什么？

1 石牛_____。

2 夏小红_____。

3 谢丽_____。

4 包健_____。

5 白雪_____。

6 王丽眉_____。

7 张朋山_____。

8 万秋花_____。

9 车老师_____。

10 李超_____。

11 李小巧_____。

12 Add your own

天气好的时候，你常做什么？

11.4 Activity Review 2

天气不好的时候，人们在家里做什么？

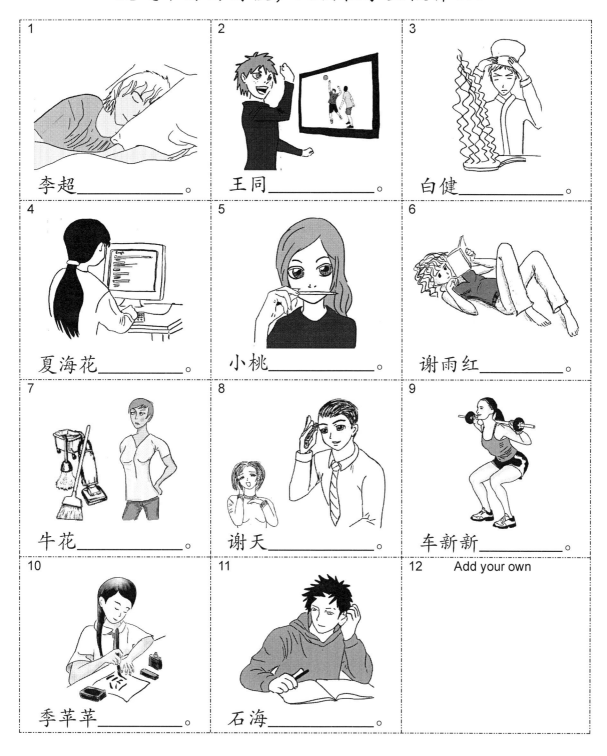

1 李超_____。

2 王同_____。

3 白健_____。

4 夏海花_____。

5 小桃_____。

6 谢雨红_____。

7 牛花_____。

8 谢天_____。

9 车新新_____。

10 季苹苹_____。

11 石海_____。

12 Add your own

天气不好的时候，你常做什么？

11.5 Ways of Transportation

他们怎么去学校？

1	2	3
马丽 _____ 。	白秋花 _____ 。	金大川 _____ 。
4	5	6
牛星星 _____ 。	石小红 _____ 。	李小巧 _____ 。
7　Add your own	8　Add your own	9　Add your own

Work in pairs.

你怎么来学校？

我骑车。

二十分钟吧。

走路，你呢？

要骑多长时间？

11.6 Work in pairs.

你那儿天气怎么样？

特好！
不冷不热，秋高气爽。
你那儿呢？

不太好。
阴天，要下雨了。

你打算做什么？

我本来要<u>去公园烧烤</u>，
现在只好在家了。
你呢？

我一会儿去跑步。

1	2	3

去海边游泳	去乡下拍照	去山上画画儿

11.7 word detective — Not so new

Here are some basic Chinese characters you have learned.
Let's see if you can decode their meanings.

	Pinyin	English	Make a sentence
1. 内心	_____	_____	_____
2. 日常	_____	_____	_____
3. 热心	_____	_____	_____

李美丽放学回到家。她坐在客厅的**沙发**上。那是一个又大又舒服的白沙发，是美丽家新买的沙发。美丽**脱**了鞋，然后把脚放在了**茶几**上。她拿起了电视**遥控器**。她把遥控器**对准**了电视。她打开了电视。美丽不想看电影，不想看**新闻**，也不想看篮球比赛什么的。美丽只想看天气**预报**，因为她特想知道明天的天气怎么样。美丽的学校明天有烧烤，所以她想知道明天的天气好不好。糟糕！天气预报说明天有雨，明天会下一天的毛毛雨！学校还会有烧烤吗？美丽有点儿担心。

第二天早上，美丽穿上了雨衣，穿上了雨鞋走出家门。美丽站在家门口，怎么没下雨呢？美丽**抬头**看了看天：天特别蓝，没有云，太阳照着，没有下下雨的样子。而且，天上还有很多鸟唱着歌飞来飞去。美丽回到卧室。她脱下了雨衣，脱下了雨鞋。最后，她只拿了把雨伞去学校了。美丽觉得该带把雨伞，万一下雨呢？

沙发 shāfā / sofa；脱 tuō/ to take off；

茶几 chájī / coffee table；遥控器 yáokòngqì / remote control；

对准 duìzhǔn / to aim at；新闻 xīnwén / news；抬头 táitóu / to raise head；

11.9 Fan with Chinese radicals.

A Chinese character often represents a part of history, an image, an idea, or an attitude about life.

For example, the character for prisoner is 囚. It consists of two parts:

口 (enclosure) and 人 (person). I think you get the picture.

彳	Write down the characters with 彳 in it.
彳 is related to road and walking. It is always placed on the left side.	
门	Write down the characters with 门 in it.
门 is related to door. Its position is fixed.	

11.10 Every picture tells a story- - What's yours?

Use your imagination. Write as many sentences as possible.

_____

_____

Culture Focus

1. How many time zones does China have?

_____

> You don't need to journey far to sightsee. Sometimes, you may just hop on a bus to explore what the nearest downtown has to offer.

wǎng qián zǒu zou　　dào chù kàn kan
往 前 走走，到 处 看看。

wǎng hòu zǒu zou　　sì chù zhuàn zhuan
往 后 走走，四 处 转 转。

shí zì lù kǒu　　sì miàn bā fāng
十 字 路 口，四 面 八 方，

dōng xī nán běi　　chē lái rén wǎng
东 西 南 北，车 来 人 往。

wǎng dōng zǒu yǒu yín háng shū diàn hé guǎng chǎng
往 东 走有银 行 书 店和 广 场。

wǎng xī zǒu yǒu dì tiě yóu jú hé shāng chǎng
往 西 走有地铁邮 局 和 商 场。

wǎng nán zǒu yǒu gōng yuán yī yuàn tú shū guǎn
往 南 走有公 园 医 院 图 书 馆。

wǎng běi zǒu yǒu chāo shì fàn diàn hé jiào táng
往 北 走有超 市 饭 店 和 教 堂。

wǎng qián zǒu zou　　dào chù kàn kan
往 前 走走，到 处 看看。

wǎng hòu zǒu zou　　sì chù zhuàn zhuan
往 后 走走，四 处 转 转。

shí zì lù kǒu　　sì miàn bā fāng
十 字 路 口，四 面 八 方，

dōng xī nán běi　　chē lái rén wǎng
东 西 南 北，车 来 人 往。

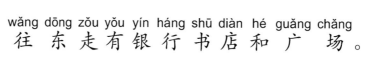

Key words

1	交通	jiāotōng	transportation
2	到处	dàochù	everywhere
3	转	zhuàn	to walk around
4	十字路口	shízìlùkǒu	intersection
5	四面八方	sìmiànbāfāng	in all directions
6	东	dōng	East
7	西	xī	West
8	南	nán	South
9	北	běi	North
10	银行	yínháng	bank
11	广场	guǎngchǎng	a public square
12	地铁	dìtiě	subway
13	邮局	yóujú	post office
14	商场	shāngchǎng	mall
15	图书馆	túshūguǎn	library
16	超市	chāoshì	super market
17	教堂	jiàotáng	church
18	迷路	mílù	to lose one's way
19	问路	wènlù	to ask for directions

Let the words flow!

nǐ zěn me qù shì nèi
你怎么去市内？

nǐ zěn me qù shàng bān
你怎么去上班？

nǐ zěn me qù jī chǎng
你怎么去机场？

nǐ zěn me qù chē zhàn
你怎么去车站？

wǒ zuò chē qù shì nèi
我坐车去市内。

wǒ zǒu lù qù shàng bān
我走路去上班。

wǒ dǎ chē qù jī chǎng
我打车去机场。

wǒ qí chē qù chē zhàn
我骑车去车站。

nǐ ne
你呢？

wǒ kāi chē qù shì nèi
我开车去市内，

wǒ dā chē qù shàng bān
我搭车去上班，

wǒ zuò dì tiě qù jī chǎng
我坐地铁去机场，

wǒ pǎo zhe qù chē zhàn
我跑着去车站。

Key words

1	上班	shàngbān	to go to work
2	机场	jīchǎng	airport
3	车站	chēzhàn	station (train, subway, bus)
4	打车	dǎchē	to take a taxi
5	搭车	dāchē	to get a ride
6	跑	pǎo	to run
7	直走	zhízǒu	to walk straight ahead
8	拐	guǎi	to turn (left or right or North, etc.)
9	摩托车	mótuōchē	motorcycle
10	公车	gōngchē	bus
11	电车	diànchē	trolley bus
12	火车	huǒchē	train
13	三轮车	sānlúnchē	rickshaw
14	船	chuán	boat; ship
15	飞机	feījī	airplane
16	票	piào	ticket
17	远	yuǎn	far
18	近	jìn	near
19	附近	fùjìn	nearby

Language Focus

12.1 Vocabulary Review.

Read it aloud. Translate it into English.
Write it in Chinese characters, and say it aloud again as you write it.

	English	**Chinese**
1. 走路去超市	_____	_____
2. 坐船回上海	_____	_____
3. 坐公车去图书馆	_____	_____
4. 没时间逛商店	_____	_____
5. 从哪儿走近?	_____	_____
6. 直走就到了。	_____	_____
7. 打车不贵。	_____	_____
8. 三个半小时以后	_____	_____
9. 东西南北中	_____	_____
10. 地铁站对面	_____	_____
11. 教堂旁边	_____	_____
12. 过马路注意车。	_____	_____
13. 站在十字路口	_____	_____
14. 往左拐就是。	_____	_____

 Big assignments should be divided into manageable chunks. Look at your calendar and work back from the due date. Figure out how much you have to do each day in order to be finished on time.

12.2 Transportation Review.

怎么去学校？

1 哥俩 _____ 。	2 夏红云 _____ 。	3 谢晴 _____ 。
4 金星 _____ 。	5 白海花 _____ 。	6 石牛 _____ 。
7 谢小歌 _____ 。	8 钱雪 _____ 。	9 包新同 _____ 。
10 李美眉 _____ 。	11 高老师 _____ 。	12 Add your own

Work in Pairs

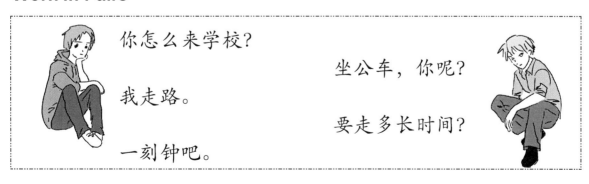

你怎么来学校？

我走路。

一刻钟吧。

坐公车，你呢？

要走多长时间？

12.3 Vocabulary Review: Places in town.

1. 想看书可以去图书馆借，可是为什么人们还要买书呢？

2. 你家附近有什么？ _____

12.4 Work in pairs.

There are many ways to give directions. One common way to give direction is to give the name of the street and some nearby building.

Asking for directions 1

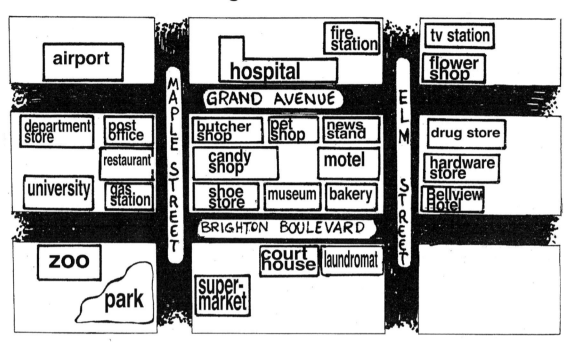

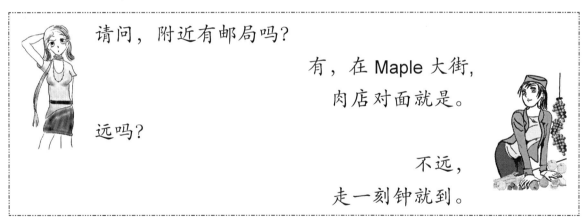

请问，附近有邮局吗？

有，在 Maple 大街，
肉店对面就是。

远吗？

不远，
走一刻钟就到。

1	2	3	4 Add your own
饭店	宠物店	花店	

Asking for directions 2

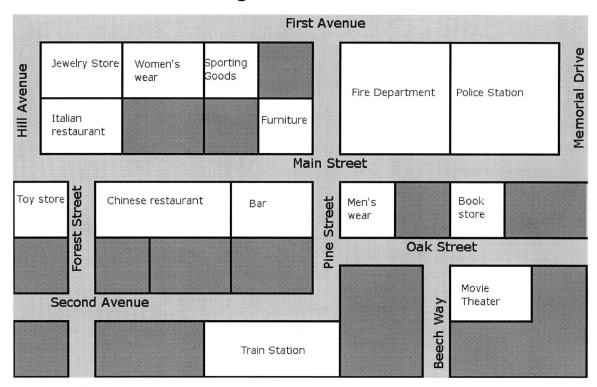

请问，**书店**怎么走？

出了火车站朝右走，
走到 Oak 路右拐，
书店在你左边，
电影院对面。

用坐车吗？

不用坐，
走两分钟就到。

1	2	3 Add your own
意大利饭店	警察局	

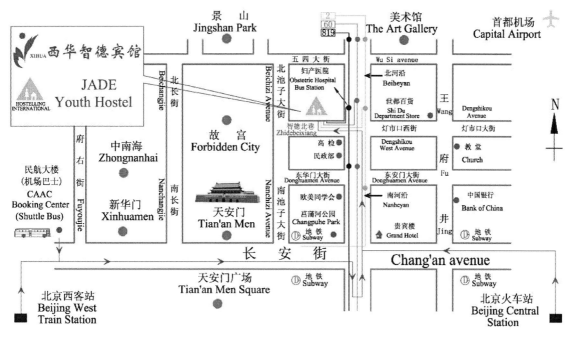

Please Take Me To JADE International Youth Hotel!

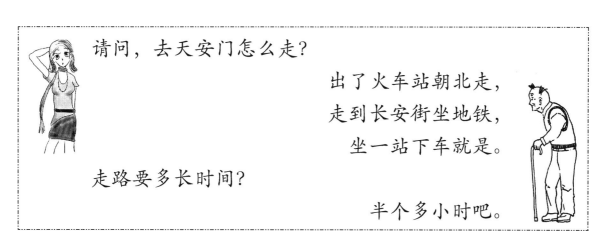

请问，去天安门怎么走？

出了火车站朝北走，
走到长安街坐地铁，
坐一站下车就是。

走路要多长时间？

半个多小时吧。

1	2	3 Add your own
教堂	景山公园	

12.5 Fill in the blanks according to the map.

北京王府井全聚德烤鸭店行车示意图

台湾饭店　和平宾馆

东安门大街　　金鱼胡同

东市安场

王府饭店

百货大楼

全聚德

校尉胡同

南河沿大街

王府井步行街

帅府园胡同

中国照相馆

工艺美术大厦

协和医院

东单北大街

东单三条

新华书店

东方广场

北京饭店

东方新天地

东长安街

市政府　　商务部　　东单体育场

1. 中国照相馆在＿＿＿＿＿＿＿＿＿＿对面。

2. 有名的北京饭店在＿＿＿＿＿＿＿＿＿＿上。

3. 王府井大街是一条＿＿＿＿＿＿＿＿＿＿。

4. 新华书店在王府井大街和＿＿＿＿＿＿＿＿的拐角处。

5. 王府饭店不在王府井大街上，在＿＿＿＿＿＿＿＿。

6. 请注意：你不可以在＿＿＿＿＿＿＿＿＿＿开车。

7. 这是一张＿＿＿＿＿＿＿＿＿＿＿＿＿＿。

12.6 word detective Not so new.

Here are some basic Chinese characters you have learned.
Let's see if you can decode their meanings.

	Pinyin	**English**	**Make a sentence**
1. 交友	_____	_____	_____
2. 行人	_____	_____	_____
3. 电子票	_____	_____	_____
4. 问路	_____	_____	_____

12.7 Fun with Chinese radicals

A Chinese character often represents a part of history, an image, an idea, or an attitude about life. Many ideas, thoughts and feelings are expressed by combining two or more characters to form a new word. In that way, each Chinese character is like a Lego brick.

For example, the character for no is 否. It consists of two parts:

不 (no) and 口 (mouth). It means the mouth says NO.

It is said that every Chinese character contains a picture. So, use your imagination when studying Chinese characters. Have fun!

辶	Write down the characters with 辶 in it.
辶 is related mostly to walking, and its position is fixed.	
土	Write down the characters with 土 in it.
土 is related to soil, and it is usually placed on the left or the bottom.	

12.8 Every picture tells a story—What's your story?

Use your imagination. Write as many sentences as you can.

后座司机

_____

_____

_____

_____

_____

_____

_____

_____

Culture Focus

1. What is the most popular form of transportation in China? _____

2. What makes a city great? _____

入乡要问俗，

入国要问禁。

如果你在中国住，

学做中国人：

送礼别送钟和鞋，

吃梨不能分。

客人来了沏杯茶，

递上热毛巾。

双手递茶水，双手递名片，

浅茶，满酒，整盒烟，

照我说的办。

客人送你礼物，

别当面打开看。

放一边，道声谢：

谢兄弟，你太客气！

谢师傅，太麻烦你！

谢先生，谢夫人，

请请请，谢谢谢，

请请，谢谢，请请，谢！

Key words

1	入乡	rùxiāng	to enter a countryside or a country
2	风俗	fēngsú	custom
3	禁	jīn	taboo
4	如果	rúguǒ	if
5	送礼	sònglǐ	to give a gift
6	沏茶	qīchá	to make tea
7	递	dì	to hand over
8	毛巾	máojīn	towel
9	名片	míngpiàn	name card
10	满	mǎn	full
11	整	zhěng	whole
12	烟	yān	cigarette
13	照办	zhàobàn	to follow the rules
14	当面	dāngmiàn	in someone's presence; in front of someone
15	道谢	dàoxiè	to express gratitude
16	师傅	shīfu	master; skilled worker
17	麻烦	máfan	to bother; troublesome
18	先生	xiānsheng	Mr.; Sir
19	夫人	fūren	Mrs.; Madam

Let the words flow!

nǐ cháng guò kǎo yā méi yǒu　　nǐ yòng guò kuài zi méi yǒu
你 尝 过 烤 鸭 没 有?你 用 过 筷 子 没 有?

nǐ fàng guò biān pào méi yǒu　　nǐ pá guò cháng chéng méi yǒu
你 放 过 鞭 炮 没 有?你 爬 过 长 城 没 有?

dào xiàn zài hái méi yǒu
到 现 在 还 没 有。

dào xiàn zài hái méi yǒu
到 现 在 还 没 有。

tóng xué men　　wǒ wèn nǐ
同 学 们,我 问 你:

gǔ lǎo de zhōng guó zài nǎ lǐ
古 老 的 中 国 在 哪 里?

lǎo shī lǎo shī ràng wǒ shuō
老 师,老 师,让 我 说:

yáo yuǎn de dōng fāng yǒu zhōng guó
遥 远 的 东 方 有 中 国。

tóng xué men　　zǐ xì kàn
同 学 们,仔 细 看:

zhōng guó dì tú xiàng gōng jī
中 国 地 图 象 公 鸡。

jī tóu cháo dōng wěi cháo xī
鸡 头 朝 东,尾 朝 西。

dōng yǒu hǎi dōng hǎi huáng hǎi rì běn hǎi
东 有 海:东 海,黄 海,日 本 海。

xī yǒu shān gāo gāo de xǐ mǎ lā yǎ shān
西 有 山:高 高 的 喜 马 拉 雅 山。

wǔ shí liù gè mín zú zhù zài zhōng jiān
五 十 六 个 民 族 住 在 中 间。

wǔ shí liù gè mín zú zhù zài zhōng jiān
五 十 六 个 民 族 住 在 中 间。

Key words

1	过	guò	marker for past perfect tense
2	筷子	kuàizi	chopsticks
3	放	fàng	to let go; to set off; to release
4	鞭炮	biānpào	fireworks
5	爬	pá	to climb
5	长城	chángchéng	Great Wall
7	古老	gǔlǎo	ancient
8	遥远	yáoyuǎn	far-away
9	东方	dōngfāng	East
10	仔细	zǐxì	careful; carefully; attentive
11	像	xiàng	to look like; to appear; to seem
12	公鸡	gōngjī	rooster
13	朝	cháo	towards; facing
14	尾	wěi	tail
15	民族	mínzú	nationality; ethnic group
16	汉族	hànzú	the Han ethnic group
17	文化	wénhuà	culture
18	地理	dìlǐ	geography
19	民俗	mínsú	customs

Language Focus

13.1 Vocabulary Review.

Read it aloud. Translate it into English.
Write it in Chinese characters, and say it aloud again as you write it.

	English	**Chinese**
1. 入乡要问俗。	_____	_____
2. 不能分梨吃。	_____	_____
3. 给客人沏茶。	_____	_____
4. 双手递名片	_____	_____
5. 照老师说的做。	_____	_____
6. 送新年礼物	_____	_____
7. 当面道谢	_____	_____
8. 多民族国家	_____	_____
9. 遥远的东方	_____	_____
10. 古老的中国	_____	_____
11. 尝尝我做的菜。	_____	_____
12. 没见过鞭炮	_____	_____
13. 到现在还没有。	_____	_____
14. 朝东走	_____	_____

 Who decides what is polite and what is not? How might rules of politeness change over time? Can you give an example?

13.2 The past perfect tense in Chinese.

过 is used to talk about past experience, something that has happened to you before.

Affirmative sentence: ......verb + 过
　　　　　　　　　　我去过中国。 I've been to China.

Question: 1)　...... verb + 过......吗?
　　　　　　　　你去过中国吗? Have you been to China?

　　　　　　2)　...... verb + 过 ......没有?
　　　　　　　　你去过中国没有? Have you been to China?

　　　　　　3)　...... verb + 没 verb 过......?
　　　　　　　　你去没去过中国? Have you been to China?

Answer: 1)　我去过中国。 I've been to China.

　　　　2)　我没（有）去过中国。 I've never been to China.

1. " Have you watched "Star War" movie? "　　" No, I haven't. "

_____

2. I have read this novel twice.

_____

3. Have you been to Shanghai? I heard it is prettier than New York.

_____

4. I've told you not to wait till the last minute to do your homework.

_____

5. I have visited that place before; however, I cannot remember a thing.

_____

13.3 中国地图

回答问题:

1. 大熊猫住在哪儿? _____

2. 中国有多少个民族? _____

3. 东三省是哪三个省? _____

4. 中国西部高,西部有什么? _____

5. 中国东部低,东部有什么? _____

6. 中国两个最大的节日是: _____

7. 汉语是谁的语言? _____

8. 中国有几个邻国-neighbors? _____

13.4 Learn about China

	省 shěng / **Province**	省会 shěnghuì / **Capital**	有什么？
1	黑龙江		
2	吉林		
3	辽宁		
4	河北		
5	河南		
6	山东		
7	陕西		
8	江苏		
9	河南		
10	河北		
11	浙江		
12	四川		
13	云南		
14	西藏		
15	福建		
16	新疆		
17	广东		
18	海南		

13.5 Food & Weather: Are they related?

	什么地方?	天气
南 甜		
北 咸		
东 辣		
西 酸		

13.6 中国文化知多少?

1. 为什么不能送给中国小孩鞋? _____

2. 为什么不能送给中国老人钟? _____

3. 为什么不要当面打开礼物? _____

4. 递名片时要注意什么? _____

5. 为什么梨不可以分着吃? _____

6. 为什么中国人不喜欢"四"? _____

7. 过年你该送给中国人什么礼物? _____

8. 过年时谁送谁红包? _____

9. 为什么中国人的姓在前名在后? _____

13.7 Fan with Chinese radicals.

A Chinese character often represents a part of history, an image, an idea, or an attitude about life.

For example, the character for customs is 俗. It consists of two parts: 亻 (person) and 谷 (grains). A person who eats grains falls into the customs category.

口	Write down the characters with 口 in it.
口 resembles a square box. Characters with the 口 refers to enclosure and scope.	
火	Write down the characters with 火 in it.
火 is related to fire. Its position is very flexible.	

13.8 word detective Not so new

Here are some basic Chinese characters you have learned.
Let's see if you can decode their meanings.

	Pinyin	English	Make a sentence
1. 中国城	_____	_____	_____
2. 礼节	_____	_____	_____
3. 禁果	_____	_____	_____
4. 古人	_____	_____	_____

Sometimes when a word is needed for something new, we don't invent a new word. Instead we put old ones together and give it a new meaning. For example, the word for "telephone" is 电话, which means electric words in Chinese.

13.9 Fan with Chinese radicals.

Here are some basic radicals you have learned so far. Write characters that contain the following radicals.

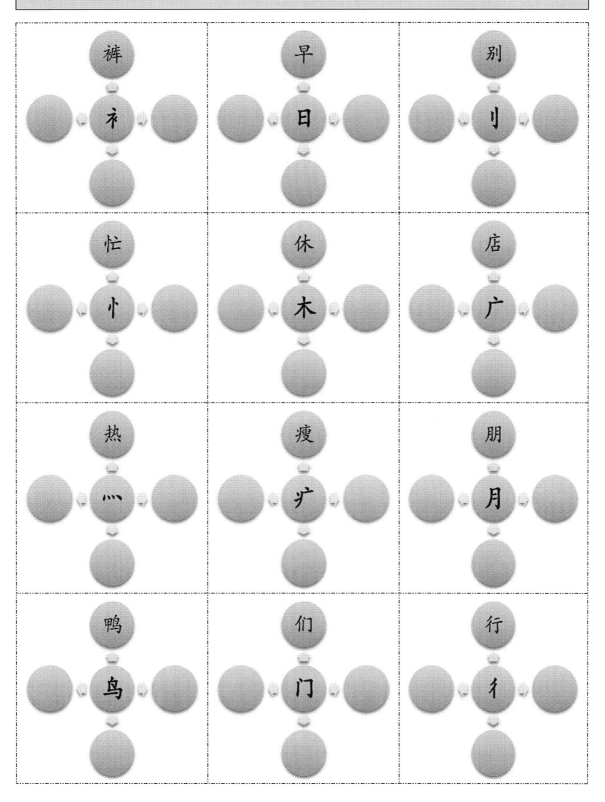

13.10 Fun with Chinese Idioms

Chinese idioms, also known as "chéngyǔ", are well defined expressions usually contain four Chinese characters. They are the heart and soul of the Chinese language, reflecting the traditions and characteristics of the Chinese culture. Look at the Chinese idioms below, and see if you can guess their meanings. Make sure to think and visualize beyond the words you read. Have fun!

Many Chinese idioms use numbers.

1. 一石二鸟　　English_____

2. 四面八方　　English_____

3. 九牛一毛　　English_____

Many Chinese idioms use parts of the body.

1. 有口无心　　English_____

2. 眼大肚子小　English_____

3. 心直口快　　English_____

Many Chinese idioms use colors.

1. 五颜六色　　English_____

2. 黑白分明　　English_____

3. 白手起家　　English_____

Many Chinese idioms use animals.

1. 狗急跳墙　　English_____

2. 笨鸟先飞　　English_____

3. 对牛弹琴　　English_____

13.11 Every picture tells a story—What's your story?

Use your imagination. Write as many sentences as you can.

Title:_____

_____

_____

_____

_____

_____

_____

_____

Culture Focus

1. Name top 2 great Chinese philosophers and their work.

_____

_____

2. Why people around the world study ancient Chinese Philosophy?

_____